CRAZY PATCHWORK

D1435674

This contemporary crazy patchwork quilt represents a lifetime of memories and will no doubt become a treasured family heirloom. It was made by Suzanne Erickson of Park Ridge, Illinois for her daughter, Lilli, a professional skater. The patches are washable materials set off by hot pink and royal blue velvet. The quilt features Lilli's hair ribbons, pieces from school uniforms and baby bassinet, embroidered Bible verses in the family's native languages, scraps from ice-show costumes, Chicago skyline, and Colorado vacation spot mementos, among others. The quilt is king size, 130" x 110" (325 cm x 275 cm).

The Complete Book of
CRAZY PATCHWORK

by Mary Conroy

A step-by-step guide to crazy patchwork projects

Sterling Publishing Co., Inc., New York

Published in 1985 by Sterling Publishing Co., Inc.
Two Park Avenue, New York, N.Y. 10016

© 1985 HYPERION PRESS LIMITED

All rights reserved. No part of this publication may be
reproduced, stored in a retrieval system, or transmitted, in
any form, or by any means, electronic, mechanical,
photocopying, recording or otherwise, without the prior
permission of Sterling Publishing Co., Inc.

Project photography by G. A. Tyler Photography; cover by
Bill Hicks Photography; historical photography credited on
relevant pages; typography by Raeber Graphics Inc.; design
& illustration by A. O. Osen; printing & binding by D. W.
Friesen & Sons, Ltd.

Printed in Canada

ISBN 0-8069-5548-1 (Trade)
ISBN 0-8069-7966-6 (Paperback)

Published by arrangement with Hyperion Press Limited,
Winnipeg, Canada.

Library of Congress No. 85-50179

ACKNOWLEDGEMENTS

I am indebted to many people for help in the preparation of this book: to Marilyn Stothers, a Winnipeg-
based quilt artist and friend who recommended me
as an authority on crazy patchwork to the publishers;
to the law firm of Conroy, Trebb, Scott, Hurtubise
and Fragomeni for assistance in the preparation of
the manuscript; to Dorothy Jacklin, friend and secre-
tary, to Mrs. Margaret Osen of Roberts, Wisconsin
and to Joyce Netzke of Sudbury, Ontario who
worked some of the projects from my designs and
gave valuable suggestions and input; to Dixie Haywood, a noted American authority on crazy patchwork in the United States whose shared expertise
over the years has been a major support in my study
of this quilt form; to Dorothy Bond whose excellent
compilation of stitches used on old American crazy
patchwork quilts never leaves my workbag; to the
Embroiderers' Guild of Canada and the Canadian
Embroiderers' Association whose support of stitchery has kept this valuable art form alive and growing
in Canada and from whom I have learned much; to
Bernice Phelps of Lakeville, New York, Suzanne
Erickson of Park Ridge, Illinois, and Beulah Hodgson
of Vancouver, Washington who responded with alac-
rity and generosity to a request from a stranger to
use their work in the book; and to many students
and friends whose work is acknowledged individually with the project directions.

Sally Garoutte of the American Quilt Study
Group and Bonnie Leman, editor of *Quilter's Newsletter* also gave valuable advice on American crazy
quilts. There are many others to whom I am grate-
ful for sharing their time and information. I thank
all of them.

And finally I cannot express in words my grat-
itude to my husband Ted, and to my children Sarah
Jane, Jamie, and Charles who made many meals for
themselves, went on excursions without me, and
who constantly lent their support, critical acclaim,
and enthusiasm to this project. I hope everyone will
be pleased with the result of my work.

CONTENTS

INTRODUCTION

"Crazy patchwork," "crazy work," "crazypatch," or "Saratoga work" are some of the names given to a particular type of needlework that is generally included in the broad category of "quilting." The most popular name for this type of work is "crazy patchwork."

Crazy patchwork is composed of irregular pieces of material of all shapes, sizes, and colors and the pieces are usually of different types of materials as well. The pieces are sewn together so that the design appears to be accidental and random. There are several methods used to sew the pieces together and the different stitches help to give the work its individuality. Although crazy patchwork can be used on a variety of household items its most common use is for a quilt top. Its history is long and varied.

Some quilt authorities believe that the earliest type of *North American patchwork* quilt was the crazy quilt.[1] They believe it developed when the original bedcoverings that the settlers had brought with them to the new land became worn. I believe that many styles and types of quilts from different countries made their way to North America with immigrants from many countries. Since the quilts could not easily be replaced the old ones were patched and kept in service. Bits of good materials, usually salvaged from the best parts of worn clothing, were sewn onto the worn areas. The patches were irregular in shape and size and many different colors and fabrics were used. Sometimes this created a rather bizarre appearance which was aptly referred to as crazy patchwork.

As patches were added from time to time the original top of the quilt was eventually covered and the end result was a crazy patchwork quilt. As the old patched quilts wore out the crazy patchwork style was retained in new quilts that were made. The patchwork style was popular partly because fabric was costly and scarce in North America for many years; the first commercial fabric mill was opened in 1815 in the United States and in 1845 in Canada. Patches were no longer sewn onto an existing quilt. Rather, the pieced layer of material was sewn to another layer of material for strength or the individual pieces were sewn directly onto a sheet or worn blanket. Because of the scarcity of material, scraps left from the making of clothing were saved as they fell from the scissors. Not even the tiniest scrap of material was wasted.[2] When new quilts were needed out came the dressmaking scraps to take their place in the new quilt creation.[3]

Early North American crazy patchwork quilts were more utilitarian than ornamental. Pioneers of that era did not have access to many fine materials nor did they have time for long hours of elaborate embroidery. These early quilts were stitched mainly with herringbone and/or featherstitching. This type of quilt is still made today in rural areas of North America.

Many quilt historians believe that crazy patchwork preceded the geometric form of patchwork in North America. One of these, British quilt authority Averil Colby in *Patchwork* states that crazy patchwork was popular because the quilt maker could make use of so many different kinds of materials — scraps of woolens, satins, silks, cottons, linens, whatever was at hand — and incorporate them all in one piece of work and still have a presentable product. Since the

1. Patsy and Myron Orlofsky, *Quilts in America* (McGraw Hill, New York, 1974), p. 299.
2. Ibid., p. 299.
3. Adelaide Hechtlinger, *American Quilts, Quilting and Patchwork* (Stackpole Books, Harrisburg, Pa., 1974), p. 16.

scraps could be of any shape or size every remnant would be put to use.[4] None of these early utilitarian pieces survive.

What is known to quilt makers today as *Victorian crazy patchwork* grew up in the Victorian age. This description is found in the *Encyclopedia of Victorian Needlework.*[5]

> *Crazy* made with pieces of silk, brocade, and satin of any shape or size. The colors are selected to contrast with each other; their joins are hidden by lines of herringbone, coral, and featherstitch worked in bright-colored filosells, and in the centres of pieces of plain satin or silk, flower sprays in satin stitch are embroidered.
>
> *To work* Cut a piece of ticking the size of the work, and baste down on it all descriptions of three-cornered, jagged, and oblong pieces of material. Show no ticking between these pieces, and let the last laid piece overlap the one preceding it. Secure the pieces to the ticking by herringbone, buttonhole, and featherstitch lines worked over their raw edges, and concealing them. Ornament them with cross-stitch, tête de boeuf, point de riz, and rosettes if the patches are small; upon large plain patches work flower sprays or single flowers in colored silk embroidery.

Jean Dubois, writing in *Quilter's Newsletter,* believes that crewel embroidery on wool which was popular in England during the late 18th century was probably the ancestor of what is known today as "Victorian crazy patchwork."[6] When this stitching was applied to quilt making, the quilters used pieces of gorgeous dress materials such as silks, satins, brocades, velvets, plushes, taffetas, and other fine woolen and calicoes as backgrounds for their fancy stitches. Because these materials were delicate they had to be attached to a firm foundation for the quilt to be of any practical use. Popular foundation materials in England were unbleached calico, sheeting, or cretonne. Various embroidery stitches in lustrous cotton, silk, and later rayon threads were used to attach the pieces and the many different patches, with their embellishments, made up the entire crazy patchwork top.

This Victorian crazy patchwork quilting became known in England around the middle of the 19th century. As far as is known no examples of the work exist that were made before 1830.[7] The first Victorian crazy quilts were sheet size (90" by 100" or 225 cm by 250 cm). Wool and linen were used for the patches as well as sumptuous silks, satins, velvets, and other fine fabrics. The patches were neatly joined and the seams were hidden by elaborate embroidery. As time passed and quilting became more popular some quilts were made in blocks or panels for ease in working. Often the repetition of colors and materials in the blocks helped to create a more symmetrical, ordered look. The blocks were joined edge to edge and these seams were also covered with a variety of embroidery stitches. Some crazy quilts had velvet, silk, or some other fancy stripping to set off the blocks.

The embroidery stitches, worked very freely and rhythmically along the seams in various stitch combinations, formed the basic structure and flavor of crazy patchwork quilts. This seam embroidery was, in fact, the unifying component in the design of the quilt and to this end worked best when the embroidery thread was all the same color. Often the choice of thread color was gold and this gave the quilt a rich look. When embroidery was used to create

4. Averil Colby, *Patchwork* (B. T. Batsford Ltd., London, 1958), p. 67.

5. S. A. Caulfield and B. E. Seward, *Encyclopedia of Victorian Needlework,* Vol. II (Dover Publications, New York, 1972), p. 381.

6. Jean Dubois, *Quilter's Newsletter* (November, 1977), p. 8.

7. Averil Colby, op. cit., p. 67.

pictures of flowers, animals, household objects, birds, people, or anything else the maker desired, this also added a distinctive look to the creation. Names and dates were often included — a practice adopted if more than one person worked on the quilt. Sometimes the maker would embroider the initials of the donors of the patches onto the material. Dates — when the quilt was started and finished — were also worked onto one of the patches, usually in a corner of the quilt. Women in those days traded left-over pieces of dress material as avidly as youngsters today trade baseball cards. This gave women of moderate circumstances a chance to create quilts from a great variety of fabrics and allowed all women to seek different and unusual materials. In fact, trading quilting samples was itself a social activity.

If the quilt maker found that a piece of material was too plain but was intended for use anyway it was not unusual that the stitcher would add a motif of colored glass beads, oil painting on the cloth, or some elaborate stitchery. Some ambitious makers even embroidered the design of printed materials for further embellishment. Novelties were also introduced. An artistic woman might sketch in India ink on plain silk or satin or she might print verses, often from the Bible, on the patches.

In North America featherstitching was the most commonly used stitch to hold the pieces together and this was closely followed in popularity by the herringbone stitch. These stitches showed numerous variations depending on the taste and skill of the maker. Eventually the stitches were used not only to cover the raw edges of the patches and hold them together but also to ornament the quilt and give it a distinctive appearance. There was no end to the imagination and ingenuity that individual quilters used to produce their products and indeed quilts often reflected individual talents and interests.

By the mid 1890s crazy patchwork quilt making became so innovative, especially in North America, that advertisements, labels, fair prize ribbons, campaign ribbons, souvenir scarves and handkerchiefs, lithographs on silk, or polychrome silk badges, and even cigar labels were used as patches. Such individual statements by quilters ensured that no two quilts were alike. This very individuality reflected time and place and way of life. Because of this, some authorities believe that crazy patchwork quilts are truly folk art.

As the crazy patchwork quilt became more elaborate its use became more ornamental — even in North America. After all that work the maker was anxious to show off her prowess with the needle and was not so concerned with the quilt's utilitarian potential. Besides, by this time the household usually had enough quilts to be used as bedcovers. Crazy patchwork quilting became more of an art for leisure hours. Stitching on the quilts became so varied that some makers considered it a point of pride to include at least one hundred stitch variations in their work. Thus the crazy patchwork quilt became a parlor throw — ostensibly intended to be drawn over a person taking a nap, but actually draped over the back of the sofa to better display the maker's handiwork. Other pieces of crazy patchwork were used as tablecloths, wall hangings, lambrequins (short fitted drapes like a valence for windows, mantles, and shelves). Still others were used as drapes that hung in the archway between the parlor and the dining room. Antimacassars, piano covers, and lampshades were also made of crazy patchwork. Smaller pieces were turned into book covers, reticules, and workbags to hold crazy patchwork in progress. In fact, if anything could be covered with fabric someone was sure to cover it with crazy patchwork.

Although crazy patchwork quilts have the name "quilt" the nature of the work makes it nearly impossible to quilt through the elaborate top, filling, and

These two crazy quilt samples (photographs this page) are owned by the Seneca Falls Historical Society in Seneca Falls, New York. They were exhibited at the Finger Lakes Bicentennial Quilt Show in 1976. The quilts were probably made in the Seneca Falls area in the last quarter of the 19th century but the name of the maker is not known. The first quilt features embroidered pictures in the centre of each block. The patches are silks and satins enhanced with stitchery around each patch. The maker utilized the hanging diamond layout of blocks set apart by narrow black strips. The edging is hand knit ecru cotton lace with a fringe. The second quilt is made up of blocks in a hexagon shape, also set apart by narrow black strips. The similarity of materials and design suggest that the two quilts were made by the same person.

Opposite, top left: Crazy patchwork was used by pioneers to dress up a simple log cabin. This shelf lambrequin was made in the late 1800s and was photographed in the Grey County Museum at Owen Sound, Ontario.

Opposite, top right: This "cigarette silk" was one of many different motifs produced as premiums by the Imperial Tobacco Company during the years 1910 to 1925. Women liked to include these pieces in crazy quilts and although they disliked smoking by the men in their lives they were persuaded to allow it because they wanted to collect the premiums.

Middle photographs: These quilts are in the collection of Dixie Haywood of Pensacola, Florida, and appear in her book The Contemporary Crazy Quilt Project Book, *Crown Publishers, New York (1977). The first is a twelve-block Victorian quilt bordered on three sides with velvet. The second is a nine-block Victorian quilt, dated "86-93" in embroidery.*

This crazy patchwork quilt (opposite, bottom photographs) is now owned by Bernice Phelps of Lakeville, New York. The quilt was made by her great-grandmother, Allison Craig, in the later part of the 19th century and was passed to her grandmother, Alice Foster, and then to Bernice Phelps. The quilt is made from silk and satin patches. The original did not have backing and the present satin backing was sewn on by Bernice Phelps' daughter, Alice.

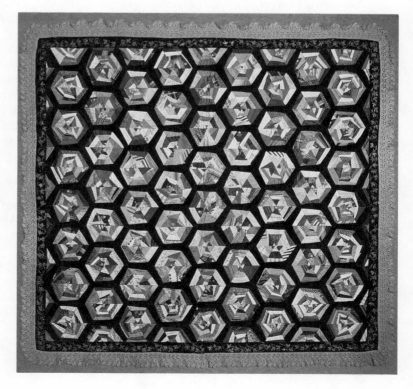

back. Occasionally one sees a quilted crazy patchwork piece but the quilting stitches are invariably large and coarse. Usually crazy patchwork quilts were tied with crochet or embroidery cotton in a color harmonizing with the backing. The tying ranged from a simple square knot to elaborate French knots and other fancy types of tufting. I have seen many variations but the most unforgettable was a quilt that featured narrow puce-colored ribbons tied in dainty bows to hold the top and lining together.

In North America when crazy patchwork quilts were made to act strictly as quilts they had either wool or cotton batting fill for warmth. Sometimes a well worn blanket was used. Usually it was quilted to the backing only, using the ocean wave, fan, or chevron quilting motif. The crazy patchwork top was then tacked on. In rural areas feedbags were washed and bleached and used for quilt backing. But if materials were very scarce the backing itself was often made of patches — pieced together feedbags or any other scraps that were available. Although many Victorian crazy patchwork quilts were padded and quilted in this way, I have seen more Canadian-made Victorian crazy patchwork quilts with this warm fill than those made in the United States. Possibly there was a greater need for warmth in the northern climate. Some of the crazy patchwork quilts I have seen are reversible. One in the Prince Edward County Museum at Picton, Ontario in Canada is made entirely of velvets in dark colors on both sides and is padded and quilted.

The majority of crazy quilts that have been preserved show colors that dominated the fashions of the era in which the quilt was made. Rich browns, a light brown called "buff," deep purple, red, maroon, kelly green, royal blue, dove gray, puce, and mauve are colors that predominated in the Victorian era. Smaller amounts of less practical colors were also included for contrast. I have seen quilts of bright and subdued colors that had edges finished with a border of knitted or crocheted lace, fringes, scallops, ruffles, and narrow binding. According to Averil Colby, "gathered-on pleated frills finished off innumerable quilts from about 1850 onwards; they are found in abundance . . . on those (quilts) made of crazy work."[8]

Victorian crazy patchwork is occasionally referred to as "oriental mosaic work" (Godey's Lady's Book, 1885) and this is the name that was current in that era. The Encyclopedia of Victorian Needlework indicates that another name was "puzzle,"[9] while Robert Bishop quotes a Victorian author who called it "Japanese piece work."[10] In the Museum at Goderich, Ontario in Canada there is a Victorian crazy patchwork quilt labeled "Saratoga work." This may have been a local appellation that stuck when some woman on vacation at Saratoga (then a fashionable resort in New York state) saw the work being done locally and referred to it as "Saratoga work" when she got home.

Victorian crazy patchwork reached its zenith in North America about 1890 but crazy patchwork continued to be made in quantities well into the early 1900s, especially in Canada and some of the northern United States. An advertisement by J. L. Potter of New York City which appeared in Godey's Lady's Book in 1885 reflects the popularity of crazy patchwork.

> Crazy patchwork We send ten samples, pieces of elegant silk, all different and cut out so as to make a diagram showing how to put them together, and a variety of new stitches, for 35 cents. We send a set of thirty-five perforated patterns, working size, of birds, butterflies, bugs, beetles,

8. Ibid., p. 68.

9. S. A. Caulfield and B. E. Seward, op. cit., p. 381.

10. Robert Bishop, New Discoveries in American Quilts (New York, 1975), p. 115.

spider's web, reptiles, Kate Greenaway figures, flowers, etc., with material for transferring to silk for 60 cents.[11]
Since *Godey's Lady's Book* reached a wide audience in the United States and Canada I expect many patterns and crazy pieces were ordered.

Agnes Miall, writing in *Patchwork: Old and New* (1937), attributed the popularity of crazy patchwork in England to the increased leisure that many women enjoyed. Since industrial machinery had taken over many of the arts and crafts formerly done in the home, baking, brewing, spinning, weaving, and clothes making were no longer duties of the housewife. Increasingly servants, who were plentiful and cheap, took over the remaining household chores. Women had fewer home activities to occupy their time and careers outside the home were unheard of. How could women fill the empty hours? Since most young women had very little money other than the dress allowance handed out by fathers and husbands, they could not be very adventurous. Thus crazy patchwork was devised by "useless women to fritter away the long, boring days."[12]

I think Mrs. Miall's view is somewhat narrow. Although many Victorian Englishwomen undoubtedly did crazy patchwork as relief from boredom, other women, particularly in North America, were delighted with the work and used it as an expression of their creative talents. Many crazy patchwork creations became virtually a family album full of snippets of family memories, and they were treasured by their descendants. In fact, inventive North American women, using their sound knowledge of embroidery stitches and their native sense of color and design, soon made a household necessity a work of art.

When traveling through Canada and the United States gathering information about crazy patchwork quilts, tracing their provenance, listening to stories about individual quilts, and being fascinated by the histories of the makers I found that many of these quilts were put together during a time of great stress in the maker's life — a husband away at war, a new bride in a strange town, a pastime for someone confined to bed. Perhaps that was the origin of the saying "a needle in the hand is worth two in another place." Our great-grandmothers were instinctively aware of the therapeutic nature of quilt making.

Men and women today marvel at the enormous amount of work that was put into these quilts and often this is the main reason for their preservation. It has always surprised me that some quilt authorities profess to find crazy patchwork quilts ugly and worthy of little praise. Jonathan Holstein, in his book *The Pieced Quilt: An American Design Tradition* says that "the design is cluttered, incoherent . . ." and describes the quilt as "useless as a cover and impossible as design and it took hundreds of hours to make."[13] Holstein maintains that these quilts embodied the "rejection of simplicity and the right angles of unadorned geometric form."[14] Patsy and Myron Orlofsky, on the other hand, writing in their authoritative book *Quilts in America,* feel that the makers of crazy patchwork quilts "showed a high degree of originality in the creation of applique collages and in the use of various needlework stitches."[15]

I love Victorian-style crazy patchwork quilts. To me they are the logical extension of the earlier utility quilt for which dire necessity dictated that every

11. S. A. Caulfield and B. E. Seward, op. cit., p. 381.

12. Agnes M. Miall, "Patchwork: Old and New," *Women's Magazines Handbook,* No. 1 (London, 1937), p. 26.

13. Jonathon Holstein, *The Pieced Quilt: An American Design Tradition* (New York Graphic Society Ltd., Greenwich, Conn., 1973), p. 62.

14. Ibid., p. 62.

15. Patsy and Myron Orlofsky, op. cit., p. 62.

scrap of material the homemaker had should be saved and used. Such cherished bits were put together with love and imagination and embellished with what stitchery the maker knew or could devise. These quilts are evidence of the North American homemaker's innate desire to beautify her home.

Holstein focuses on the later Victorian desire to put as many stitches and stitch variations and combinations on the surface of the quilt as possible. For him, this cluttered fancywork was the "genteel" occupation of women who had nothing to do with their time. However, I delight in these elaborate quilts and I believe they have preserved for us a good variety of embroidery stitches which otherwise might have fallen into disuse. Dedicated stitchers today often refer to these old Victorian crazy patchwork quilts for inspiration in stitching.[16]

Detractors of the crazy patchwork quilt frequently charge that the principles of design such as balance, rhythm, repetition, and symmetry are ignored. But I think that most examples of the work are evidence of the maker's careful placement of patches so that colors and textures form a pleasing whole.

Most women in North America in the 19th century made at least one quilt every winter. Often it was crazy patchwork. The box of pieces came out after Christmas, certain pieces were selected, and the stitching began. Some crazy patchwork quilts were a family effort; others were the work of groups of women who met for company or who made a quilt for some community project. Since there were no paper patterns to follow and no stipulation about size of patches or colors used, each design depended on the eye of the maker. These expressions of individual taste were unique and to my mind worthy.

Crazy patchwork quilts continued to be popular across North America until sometime after 1914. They can still be found at auctions, estate sales, and through antique dealers, but they are becoming scarce and expensive. Most of the very elaborate, lovingly created works are still in the hands of the descendants of the makers. They are treasured for their emotional ties as well as for their intrinsic beauty.

Both of these quilts belong to the Minnesota Historical Society. The first is noteworthy for the lace-like quality of the stitchery. The second was made for the first Winter Carnival in St. Paul. It features a detail of stumpwork (the castle) with rhinestone stars at the centre of the quilt. (Photos taken by Patricia Cox.)

16. Martha Davenport, "Inspiration from a Crazy Quilt," *Needle Arts*, Vol. XII, No. 3 (Summer, 1981), p. 9.

Crazy patchwork has several parts: a foundation upon which the pieces are stitched, decorative patches, decorative stitching, backing or lining, and inter-lining (padding) if desired and appropriate to the article being made.

Components of Crazy Patchwork

The Foundation

The purpose of the foundation is twofold: to give the fine fabrics strength and durability and to provide a base upon which to sew the patches.

You can use unbleached, preshrunk (factory) cotton, worn sheets (the good parts), or any lightweight, sturdy fabric. Even printed fabric is acceptable since it will not be seen when the work is complete.

The foundation may be cut into squares or panels, but be sure to allow about 2″ (5 cm) extra all around the piece because the stitching tends to "take up" considerable fabric. The foundation materials should be preshrunk and pressed before starting to work. Keep all the pieces flat as you sew, otherwise the pieces may buckle and the patchwork will look uneven. To prevent this from happening you may wish to work the stitches in an embroidery hoop.

Decorative Patches

You may use any kinds of materials that you like to put together provided you intend to have the product dry cleaned. Otherwise consider the washability of the pieces. Begin by placing the pieces and rearrange them until you have a pleasing arrangement of colors, shapes, and textures. Traditionally, scraps were used in the shapes that fell from the scissors. However, I'm sure that great-grandma did a little snipping here and there to improve the shape and add interest to the composition. Be sure to trim away any frayed edges.

Techniques for Attaching Patches

Traditional Method   When you have a pleasing arrangement of patches pin the pieces down, underlapping and overlapping as you find they work best. Velvet is good to underlap because it is so much heavier than other fabrics. Next turn the edges under and baste them down with light-colored thread, leaving the knots on top for easy removal. *Note:* Basting is important because pins will come out and allow the patches to slip while you are doing the fancy stitching. Work your embroidery stitching next and then press the work face down on a turkish towel.

Semi-traditional Method   After assembling your collage, remove the patches, laying them out in the same order beside your sewing machine. Starting at the lower left corner with the first scrap right side up on the corner, attach the second scrap by laying it face down over the first patch, and sew the seam on the machine. Turn the material to the right side, press and pin. Continue

A *Arrange pieces in desired pattern on foundation block. Overlap and underlap as needed. Pin in place.*

B *Starting at left lower corner turn under overlapped edges and baste with running stitches. Remove pins.*

C *Basted pattern block is now ready for embroidery.*

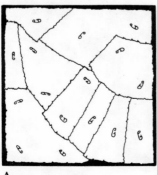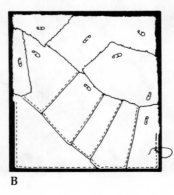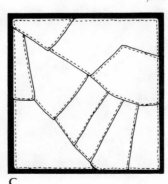

A

B

C

Traditional Method

adding pieces in this way until the block is completely covered.

You will find that there are some seams that cannot be sewn down by machine and have to be sewn down by hand. When you reach such a seam, be sure to start your machine stitching in 1/4" (0.6 cm) so that it allows you to turn under a seam allowance on the hand stitch seam. It is not necessary to sew down the raw edges along the edge of the foundation block.

You will probably find that there are tiny raw edges or gaps left in the body of the block as you sew. You may either applique a patch over them, stitch them down with an individual hand stitch using thread of the same color as the cloth, or embroider a motif over them.

Finish the block with hand embroidery. Sometimes the appearance of such a block is striking *without* all the embroidery, and you may wish to leave all or some of it off. In that case, you have just made a contemporary crazy patchwork-style block!

Semi-traditional Method with Variation I You may choose to pad each block in a kind of quilt-as-you-go technique. Prepare the foundation blocks and matching squares of *bonded* quilt batting. Bonded batting does not catch in your machine so easily. Work ahead as in the semi-traditional method. You may choose not to put hand embroidery on it but leave it as it is. If you use good material for the foundation and do not take your hand stitches right through to the backing, and if you are careful in starting and stopping your machine stitching, the work will be reversible.

Semi-traditional Method with Variation II Prepare as above but use your decorative cams or dials on the machine to do the machine embroidery. If you are skilled, you can use free machine embroidery.

Machine Method Proceed with the preliminary steps but do not underlap or overlap. Using the satin stitch on your sewing machine, completely cover the raw edges of the scraps. If you use black thread, this gives an attractive stained-glass appearance. Or, you may use up all the scraps of thread you have accumulated in a kind of *crazy stitching*. If your machine is correctly set up for satin stitching, you may use up scraps of threads of different colors on the bobbin.

Modern Materials Machine Method Using either the traditional or the semi-traditional methods you can use polyester knit materials that do not fray and omit the underlapping and overlapping. Use decorative machine stitching to attach to the foundation, being sure that the stitch chosen swings into both scrap edges securely.

A *Place first scrap right side up on the foundation block; attach second scrap by laying it face down on the first scrap and sew the seam by machine.*

B *Turn material to right side and press and pin. Continue adding pieces until the block is completely covered.*

C *If you notice tiny gaps or raw edges once you have attached all your pieces, you may applique a patch over them, stitch them down with a hand stitch, or embroider a motif over them.*

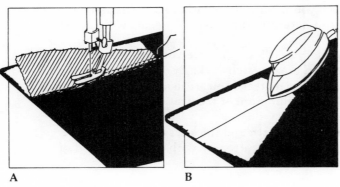
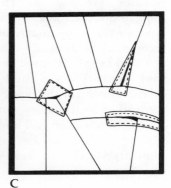

A   B   C

Semi-traditional method

Planned Crazy Patchwork This seems like a contradiction in terms but if you want every block alike or very similar you can 1) draw a crazy patchwork pattern on paper and cut the pieces for each block exactly alike or 2) make sure that you use the same materials and colors in essentially the same places in your blocks but not necessarily in the same shapes. You can then proceed to work the block.

Decorative Stitching

For stitching you can use any embroidery thread or any attractive thread. This includes stranded floss, pearl cotton in any weight, crewel yarn (especially on wool materials), fine crochet thread in any color, coton à broder, novelty threads such as those made of rayon, silk threads, velour threads, and all types of machine embroidery threads. Most of the stitching is done on and along both sides of a seamline (where one patch overlaps another). This work is done without any preliminary marking and has the great virtue of allowing you to work freely and imaginatively. See stitch instructions beginning on page 25.

Threads Any embroidery thread, in fact, any thread may be used for the stitchery. My advice is to investigate a good needlecraft shop in your area. They can supply your needs when they understand what you want and they will know about larger suppliers from whom they could order additional threads.

I like to use *DMC #5 or #8 pearl cotton thread* for the stitchery. It comes in balls in a wide range of colors and has a sheen. It is twisted to prevent the strands from separating while you work. *Crewel yarn* can also be used. It creates an entirely different feeling on silks, etc., and is gorgeous on wools. It also comes in a wide range of colors. Use a short length (12" or 30 cm) so that it does not fray as it passes in and out of the material. If you live in an isolated area your choice of colors may be governed by what you can obtain in your area or by mail order.

Crochet thread (fine) now comes in a wide range of colors and works beautifully for the stitchery. *Coton à broder,* a very soft, twisted cotton thread, may be more difficult to find but it's lovely to use. *Stranded embroidery threads* can be used but since the strands are not twisted they may leave small loops if you are not very careful. *Novelty threads* such as those made of rayon come in lovely colors but some threads are difficult to use. *Pure silk threads* are quite easy to use and very strong. They come in a wide range of colors. When working with silk threads be sure your hands are smooth. The thread catches in small rough areas on your hands rather easily. *Velour threads* are suitable mostly for couching. *Machine embroidery threads* come in cotton, polyester, and rayon. They all work well.

Needles When learning the basic group of stitches it is helpful to know something about the tools with which you will need to work. I have discussed the types of threads you may use and naturally the choice of needle will have to accommodate them.

A package of assorted embroidery needles will serve you well for most of your stitchery needs for Victorian crazy patchwork. By working with the correct needle for the type of stitch and material you are using, you will assure yourself of high-quality work with a minimum of frustration. The following are the needles you will find useful.

Sharps These needles are medium length and thickness with a small eye. They are suitable for sewing with sewing cotton or with a single strand of stranded embroidery cotton or pure silk. These needles come in different lengths. Choose the length most comfortable for you.

Crewel   These needles come in sizes 1 to 5 and 3 to 9. They are long and sharp pointed with a large eye for using six strands of stranded embroidery cotton, coton à broder, fine crochet cotton, and #8 pearl cotton. There is also a size 5 crewel needle with a much larger eye (same length usually) to accommodate tapestry wool and #5 pearl cotton. Crewel needles are the most commonly used.

Chenille   This needle is short and sharp with a large eye for thick threads, tapestry wool, and some of the softer embroidery cottons available from other countries. It is referred to as number 19. It is useful for novelty threads.

Tapestry   These needles are primarily used in the working of needlepoint. They come in several sizes. An assortment can be bought in one package. They are used for embroidery because of their blunt end and large eye. I use them for whipped and laced stitches where I need to be careful not to catch the fabric.

Milliner's   This needle is long and slender and is used with polyester and cotton sewing threads primarily for basting.

Beading   These needles are very fine and long and are used for sewing beads or sequins to your work. They bend easily and should be handled carefully.

Transferring Design Motifs

In the manner of the Victorians, plain patches may have decorative designs embroidered or beaded onto them. Many stitches are used to execute the designs. The choice is ultimately left to the imagination of the maker. However, if you do not wish to do the stitches free hand a design motif can be transferred to the pieces, although the procedure is a bit difficult.

Pouncing and pricking   The design, drawn on a piece of stiff paper or cardboard, is pricked with a darning needle. Be sure to go back and prick it through from the underside as well or the holes are blocked and the chalk will not go through. Then lay the design in the desired place, and using either talcum powder, powdered chalk, or powdered bluing (none of these should stain permanently; on some fabrics cinnamon works well, but never use cocoa because it stains) rub the powder so that it goes through the holes. Gently lift off the stencil and with a very sharp white drawing pencil, connect the dots lightly. Gently blow off the powder. This will not work on some fabrics such a velour, velvets, and velveteens.

Drawing on tissue   Draw the design accurately onto a piece of tear-away stabilizer (nonwoven materials used for making permanent patterns such as Do-Sew™ and Trace-A-Pattern™). Pin or baste the design pattern in place. Then work your embroidery through this (tissue paper will also work) and when you are finished gently pull away the stabilizer or paper. Use your tweezers to remove the last of the tiny pieces of paper.

A *Draw design on stiff paper and prick holes along the lines with a darning needle or awl.*

B *Lay stencil design on desired place and sprinkle talcum powder, powdered chalk, or powdered bluing and rub so that powder goes through the holes.*

C *Lift off and with a very sharp pencil, connect the dots lightly. Blow off powder.*

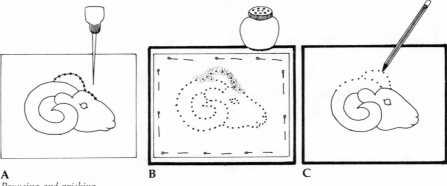

A   **B**   **C**

Pouncing and pricking

Drawing on fabric   Draw the design onto cotton organdy and baste in place. With a fine needle using a running stitch, go over the design. Gently cut away the organdy so that only the pattern stitches remain. Stitch as usual. Pull out the basting stitches at the end. *Note:* Never use typing carbon for transferring designs; it stains and smudges permanently. Check dressmaker carbon on a small scrap first. Some of these *do not come out,* even with dry cleaning or washing.

Backing (lining)   Backing is used to hide rough work and the batting. It is tacked to the batting at 12" (30 cm) intervals and should not show through to the front. Plain, non-slippery material in a dark shade to hide soil is best.

Interlining (batting)   An old quilt, blanket, wool comforter batt, or any cotton or synthetics available today work very well. Interlining provides warmth by providing a layer of insulation.

Reference Reading

Bond, Dorothy, *Embroidery Stitches From Old American Quilts,* self-published, editions 1 and 2, 34706 Row River Road, Cottage Grove, Oregon, 97424.

Boucher, Jo, *The Complete Guide to Embroidery Stitches and Crewel,* Meredith Corporation, Des Moines, Iowa, 1971.

Christie, Mrs. Archibald, *Samplers and Stitches,* B. T. Batsford Ltd., London, 1926.

Haywood, Dixie, *The Contemporary Crazy Quilt Project Book,* Crown Publishers Inc., New York, 1977. New edition, 1981.

Hen, L. R., *Needlework Designs From Old Crazy Quilts,* self-published, 224 Westminster, Tallahassee, Florida, 32304.

Houcky, Carter and Miller, Myron, *American Quilts and How to Make Them,* Scribner Co., New York, 1975.

Karasz, Mariska, *Adventures in Stitches,* Funk and Wagnall, New York, 1959, 1975.

Kretsinger, Rose G., and Hall, Carrie A., *The Romance of the Patchwork Quilt,* Bonanza Books, New York, 1935.

McKendry, Ruth, *Quilts and Other Bed Coverings in the Canadian Tradition,* Van Nostrand Reinhold Ltd., Toronto, 1979.

Miall, Agnes M., "Patchwork; Old and New," *The Women's Magazine,* London, 1937.

Orlofsky, Patsy and Myron, *Quilts in America,* McGraw-Hill Book Co., Toronto, 1974.

Peto, Florence, *American Quilts and Coverlets,* Chanticleer Press, New York, 1949.

Stafford, Carleton E., and Bishop, Robert, *America's Quilts and Coverlets,* E.P. Dutton and Company, Inc., New York, 1972.

Thomas, Mary, *Mary Thomas's Embroidery Book,* Gramercy Publishing Company, New York, 1925.

Webster, Marie D., *Quilts: Their Story and How to Make Them,* Doubleday-Page and Company, New York, 1916.

Part 2
THE STITCHES
OF CRAZY PATCHWORK

Stitches Make Work Unique

The stitching on crazy patchwork forms a complex yet unified design that melds all the components into one spectacular whole. It is one of the most important parts of the creation of a unique and lovely work and has, as well, the enjoyable characteristic that the "doer" cannot make a mistake because she is the "creator" as well. What you choose and how you choose to execute the stitch is unique — if your stitch is not quite the same as the illustration, well, perhaps you have invented a new stitch.

My personal examination of hundreds of crazy patchwork quilts establishes that the stitches used on them fall into two categories, defined by function. The first group consists of those that serve to secure the patches on either side of the join or seam. I call these *linear* stitches because they are worked along the edge of the patch in a linear fashion. These stitches must also be capable of being executed quickly as the entire surface of the work will be secured in this way.

The second group of stitches is made up of those most commonly used in rendering the "art work" or embroidered motifs which are a feature of crazy patchwork. These motifs are very personalized and have great meaning to the stitcher and/or the recipient of the work. I call these *decorative* stitches.

Do not let the names of stitches frighten you away from embroidery. They are simply a convenient way of referring to certain movements of needle and thread to create a specific result. As well, keep in mind that the same stitches have different names in different parts of the country or the world. This often results in the same name being attached to quite different stitches. Some authors organize the stitch glossary alphabetically, others by the function of the stitch. I have organized stitches in another well-recognized manner, by their "family," i.e. their similarities in execution. In most cases I have indicated whether the stitch is primarily a linear stitch or a decorative stitch for your convenience in selecting the appropriate stitch for your purpose.

According to Mrs. Archibald Christie, an early authority on embroidery techniques, the four main groups of stitches are flat, looped, chained, and knotted. In discussing each stitch family, I like to concentrate on the common characteristics and to draw your attention to the principles of the stitch. If you find you have difficulty learning a stitch, refer to the explanations of that stitch in several books. Experiment with needle, thread, and "doodle cloth" to see if someone else's explanation makes the principle of the stitch clear and allows the technique to "sink in." Reference reading materials are listed throughout the book for additional information.

For the interest of the "crazy stitcher" I include here information on the background of some of the most commonly used stitches of crazy patchwork.

The first is *featherstitch*, without a doubt the most popular stitch format on crazy patchwork quilts. It has many variations and combines well with other stitches for elaborate effects. Mrs. Christie says that featherstitch is suitable for carrying out lines or fernlike leaves and would be an appropriate method for executing any kind of light all-over pattern upon a background. It is precisely for these two qualities that stitchers choose the featherstitch. It belongs to the looped stitch family and is worked alternately on each side of the join. Some of the most common variations are double and triple featherstitch, closed featherstitch, and chained featherstitch. It works up quickly and when the stitcher establishes her own natural rhythm, any variation of the featherstitch gives a flowing, free effect which nevertheless has the effect of unifying the whole.

Herringbone stitch, also known as "catch stitch," "mussel stitch," "russian stitch," and "russian cross-stitch" is the next most commonly seen stitch. It is used extensively on the more utilitarian wool crazy quilts, especially those made in rural Ontario. Aside from its ease in working it is the most economical stitch in terms of yarn or thread required. According to *The Needle Workers Dictionary* (MacMillan, London, 1976), herringbone is "a simple interlacing stitch and is especially good for holding down raw edges, especially in fabric which does not fray." These qualities made it a popular choice for crazy patchwork. There are many variations of this stitch and it combines well with other basic stitches. Jo Boucher, writing in her book *The Complete Guide To Embroidery Stitches and Crewel* notes that this simple but effective stitch has been in use for hundreds of years in most cultures and both the regular and double herringbone stitches were extensively used in 14th-century paintings of the Last Supper by Giotto at the Arena Chapel in Padua. Some of the more commonly seen variations of this stitch are the "double herringbone," "crisscross herringbone," "laced herringbone," plaited herringbone," and "tied herring-bone" stitches.

The *outline stitch*, known also as "stem stitch" or "crewel stitch," is found frequently on heritage quilts. When used as a linear stitch, it is often made to meander so as to secure the patches on each side of the join. This gentle, regular curving also provides the perfect space for small motifs which, if repeated regularly, are most attractive. This stitch is often used in the execution of the "art work" of the crazy patchwork design, both in outline and in filling.

Another stitch, the *fern stitch*, is very attractive, works up quickly, and has a more angular appearance than the featherstitch. This flat stitch helps achieve variety by varying the proportions of the three stitches and the distances between them.

The *cretan stitch*, sometimes known as "long-armed featherstitch" or "persian stitch," is a delightfully versatile stitch for line embroidery on crazy patchwork. The most popular variation of this stitch is really a combination of the cretan and herringbone stitches. This combination gives a particularly flowing look to a line of stitching and can also form the basis of numerous other combinations (see page 40).

Fly stitches, when worked in a line vertically, also give a very angular appearance. By varying the length of the anchor or tie stitch, embroiderers can make numerous variations. The fly stitch is a looped stitch and can act as the basis for many combinations (see pages 38, 39).

Looped stitches are easy to do, fast, and very versatile. Looped stitches may be worked in the hand rather than always in a hoop. If the material is flimsy and it is difficult to keep the correct tension (or lack of it!), a temporary backing such as oilcloth or heavy, flexible plastic can be basted to the work. This is done extensively in Europe. The Scandinavian countries use birch bark.

The *buttonhole stitch* is also a looped stitch and has been used for centuries to prevent the fraying of edges and for ornamental stitching. The crazy patchwork stitcher uses it for both qualities. It works quickly and is capable of many variations (see pages 37, 38).

The *chain stitch* is a very old decorative and linear stitch that can also be used for filling and shading. It has its own category, the chain family. It is both economical of thread and time. The majority of the thread lies on top of the material. The most commonly seen variations are zigzag chain, cable chain, broad chain, chequered chain, and feathered chain (see pages 36-37). It can be used for filling and is often seen in its detached form in decorative motifs on antique crazy patchwork quilts. Jo Boucher's book lists fifty-five versions of this stitch.

Learning New Stitches

It's a good idea to practise unfamiliar stitches before you use them in your work. Do them on "doodle cloth" — some type of evenly, but loosely woven material such as monk's cloth or Aida cloth. The even weave makes it possible to count stitches to learn about spacing which is an important feature of stitchery, especially when working freely as one does in crazy patchwork embroidery. Choose a light color and a strongly contrasting #5 pearl cotton so that you can see all the details clearly. The light-colored cloth permits you to draw lines and shapes on it with a lead pencil in order to practise the appropriate spacing. Using a plastic stencil called a circlemaker (available at most stationers) draw some circles on which to practise the stitches in roundel fashion. You will use it many times when you wish to embroider a roundel on a plain patch. If the color of your material is dark, use a white art pencil; if light, use an HB lead pencil or a blue "disappearing" water marker. When the stitch is familiar you can work it on any material in your crazy patchwork and your stitches will be uniform and neat.

Some Stitch Definitions

Anchor stitch   See tie stitch.

Double   Usually refers to one line of stitching plus another immediately below it in reverse.

Interlace   Often used interchangeably with threading but also used to convey the idea of the lacing threads themelves interlocking. This may also be used from side to side as well as up and down.

Lace   See threading.

Long-armed   Used to describe the thread that anchors another, as in tie stitch, but of much greater length.

Pad   To elevate the surface of the stitching by working it over another set of stitches, often the same stitch worked in another direction, or by the use of some soft material such as string or felt.

Raise   To elevate the surface of the stitching by working it over another set of stitches, often different stitches.

Short-armed   Used to describe the anchor or tie thread but somewhere in size between a tie stitch thread and a long-armed thread.

Slipping   A small extra stitch taken through a tie or anchoring stitch.

Tie stitch   A small stitch taken to anchor or tie down a loose stitch.

Threading   To work a second thread through the stitching without piercing the material but working in an up and down direction. Usually, this is done in a contrasting color. This term is often used interchangeably with lacing and interlacing although the latter sometimes has a different connotation.

Whip   To wind a thread around a set of stitches, working always in the same direction and often with a contrasting color of thread. The second thread pierces the material only at the beginning and end of the line of stitching.

Notes on Embroidery Techniques

These simple hints will help you create beautiful patchwork.

• Stitches should be firm but not tight or puckered and should lie smoothly on top of the material. Use your thumb on your left hand to help guide the thread (if you are right-handed).

• Keep the back of your work neat. Clip threads closely and neatly.

• Do not "carry" your thread more than half an inch (1.25 cm) on the back of your work. "Carrying" contributes to puckering and the time taken to end off and start again in a new place is well worth the trouble.

• Make bigger stitches than you think you need, especially at places like points, corners, and curves where stitches seem to "shrink" a little.

• Work the inside of a shape first and outline last for the neatest effect.

• Do *not* use knots; they make bumps and sometimes pull out under wear. Instead, pick up a small number of threads with your needle and pull it through so that only a short end of the thread is left on the wrong side. Pick up about the same amount of threads on the ground fabric with your needle at a *right angle* to the previous stitch. Pull the stitch taut. This is a very neat and secure fastening. Use the same procedure at the end of your stitching. In effect, the right-angle stitch pierces the first stitch and keeps it from slipping.

Guide to Basic Stitches

I like the definition of stitches used by Mariska Karasz in her ground-breaking book, *Adventures in Stitches.* I have used her definitions as a guide. The stitches are marked suitable for *Linear* stitching or for *Decorative* motifs. Flat stitches are the simplest stitches and they form the largest category.

Flat Stitches

Out of a single flat stitch you can develop all the variations. "Flat" means that the thread always lies on the surface of the material. This is true whether the stitches are placed side by side, overlap, cross one another, or are taken backward or forward.

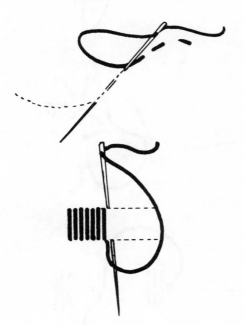

Running Stitch

Several stitches, all equal in length, are taken up on the needle. The spaces between each stitch should be equal to the length of the stitch. The stitches are worked from right to left.   *Linear*

Satin Stitch

This consists of single flat stitches taken close together with an even tension, usually filling a shape such as a leaf, a flower, etc. Start working the shape at its widest part and work to each end. This helps to keep the tension even and it is the tension of this stitch that makes it beautiful. Fill the shape with the satin stitch first and *then* outline it for best effect.   *Decorative*

Long and Short Stitch

The first row alternates long and short stitches as shown in the diagram. The following rows are made of stitches of equal length worked at the end of the long and short stitches. Start at the outer edge of the shape and work towards the centre. This stitch is mainly used for filling and shading. *Decorative*

Backstitch

Short, flat stitches are placed end to end for the slimmest outline you can achieve with embroidery stitches. Work from right to left. *Linear*

Stem Stitch

Also called "outline stitch" or "crewel stitch" this stitch can be used as a filling stitch and can be shaded quite richly. Make a sloping stitch along the line of the design or seam. Take the needle back and bring it through about halfway along the previous stitch. Work from left to right. *Linear*

Fishbone Stitch

This is used mainly for filling, especially leaves. It has quite a deep slant. Bring the thread through at 1 and make a small straight stitch along the centre line of the shape. Bring the thread through at 2 and make a sloping stitch across the base of the first stitch. Bring the thread through at 3 and make a similar sloping stitch to overlap the previous stitch. Work alternately on each side until the shape is filled. *Decorative*

Fern Stitch

This is very useful on Victorian crazy patchwork. It works nicely along the seamlines. Make flat stitches that are equal in length. It has three single stitches which radiate from a common centre. Work the three stitches and then work the next group of three. *Linear & Decorative*

Bundle or Sheaf Stitch

This stitch is composed of three equal stitches in an upright position which are then tacked down by a horizontal shorter stitch. *Linear*

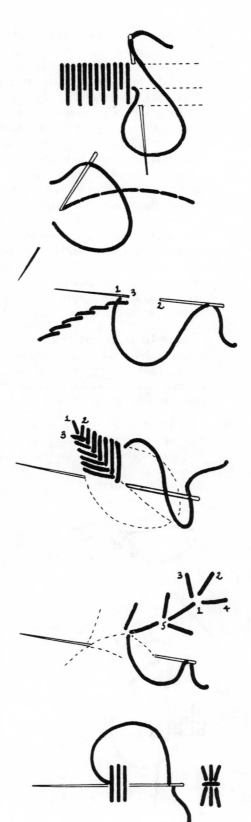

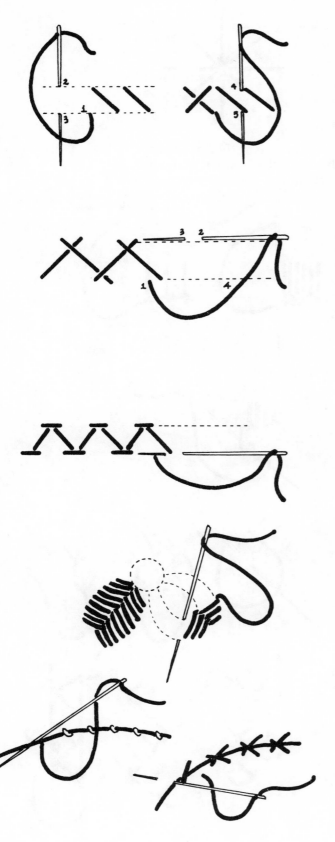

Cross-Stitch

It is important that the crosses of the entire piece be worked in the same direction. Work all the underneath threads in one direction and all the top threads in the opposite direction, keeping them as even as possible. When worked in a row, be sure to make all the crosses touch by putting your needle in the same hole as used for the adjacent stitch.   *Linear & Decorative*

Herringbone Stitch

Mentally work these stitches between two parallel lines. You may lightly draw in these lines when you first start but you will soon be working them without this aid. Bring the thread up through the lower line, insert the needle in the upper line a little to the right and take a short stitch to the left. Insert the needle on the lower line a little to the right and take a short stitch to the left. Two very good uses for this stitch are to make thick stems or to connect two solid areas for a softening effect.   *Linear*

Chevron Stitch

This is similar to the herringbone stitch but it has a straight, flat stitch marking each diagonal end. Rows of chevron stitches which touch one another make a good filling stitch.   *Linear & Decorative*

Flat Stitch

Take a small stitch alternately on each side of the shape to be filled, with the point of the needle always coming out on the outside line of the stitch. Two lines can be drawn down the centre of the shape as a guide for the size of the stitch.   *Decorative*

Couching

Lay the thread to be couched on the fabric. Using the same color thread or a contrasting one, take small stitches at even intervals over the laid thread to hold it. This stitch does not wear well and is not as suitable for crazy patchwork. If the loose "laid" thread is held down by crossing the stitches it is called a *thorn stitch*. This can be done without a frame and wears quite well.   *Linear*

Star Stitch

Work an upright cross and then a diagonal cross. The stitches are held together by a small cross-stitch at the centre. *Linear & Decorative*

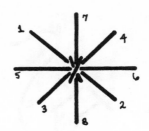

Looped Stitches

These are flat stitches which are pulled to one side by looping the thread under the point of the needle before completing it. It could well be called the "thumb" stitch as the thumb is indispensable in its execution.

Buttonhole Stitch (Blanket Stitch)

To work this stitch bring the needle up through the fabric. Holding the thread under the left thumb, form a loop and pass the needle through the fabric and over the looped thread. Work from left to right. Repeat as often as necessary. This stitch can be used to cover a raw edge or as a decorative stitch in a line. When it is used as a filling stitch, work each row into the heading of the preceding one. *Linear & Decorative*

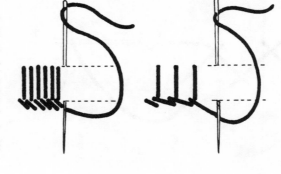

Tailor's Buttonhole Stitch

This stitch has an additional knot at the heading which gives it a firmer and more ornamental appearance. Work stitches close together. Loop the thread around the needle once before completing each stitch. *Linear & Decorative*

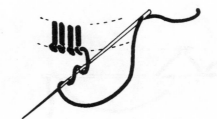

Featherstitches

Single, double, triple, and closed featherstitches are easy to make. Bring needle out at 1 and insert at 2 bringing it out again at 3. Loop the thread alternately to the right and left as you work down the seamline (A). For a double featherstitch, make two stitches at 1 and 2 (B). For a triple featherstitch, make three stitches at 1 and 2 (C). Usually the centre stitch is a bit taller than the other two.

   To make a closed stitch, instead of carrying the thread a little way to make the next stitch, keep it close to the initial stitching (D). *Linear*

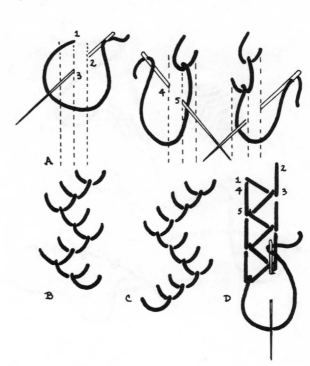

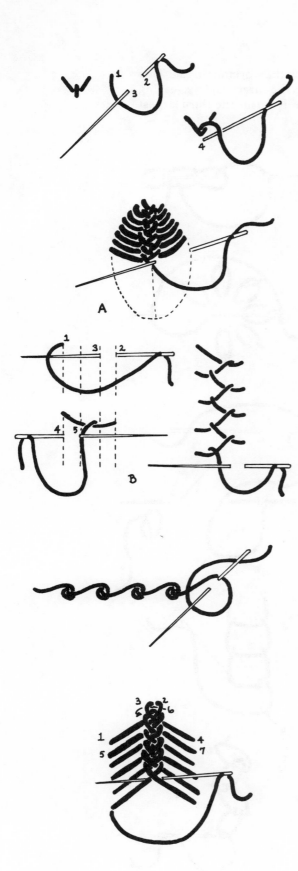

Fly Stitch
This is simply a detached featherstitch. The thread is held by the left thumb until the tiny tacking stitch is taken.
Linear & Decorative

Cretan Stitch
This is useful for working leaves and covering raw edges of patches. Bring the needle through at the apex of the leaf or the beginning of the row. Loop it under the needle and take a small stitch on the right side. Take stitches alternately on each side, always inserting the needle on the margin of the leaf or shape and bringing it back out near the centre (A). A different appearance can be created by working the stitches at an angle and making the centre portion much smaller. This can also be worked as an open cretan which is good for seams on crazy patchwork (B). Remember to keep the needle facing from right to left.   *Linear & Decorative*

Scroll Stitch
Loop the thread by throwing it first towards the right and then back to the starting point where it must be held secure by the thumb. Insert the needle in the centre of the loop and pull the thread through to complete the stitch. Work from left to right. Use a firm thread for best results.
Linear

Vandyke Stitch
This is useful for covering raw edges of patches if they are too bulky to be turned under. Trace a line a short distance on either side of the raw edge. Bring the needle through on the left traced line. Pick up a small portion of the fabric in the centre and *about 1/2" (1.25 cm) higher up.* Insert needle in the right traced line. Bring the thread across the back just below the stitch on the left side. Slip the needle *under* the loop created by the first stitch, loop it and insert on the right side. Continue.   *Linear*

Chained Stitches

The simple chain is a two-sided linear stitch, linked by the working thread. This stitch is worked vertically or horizontally and covers the suface rapidly, leaving very little thread on the reverse side. The chain family forms the third largest group of stitches and is very versatile.

Simple Chain Stitch

The thread is looped under the needle, then drawn through. Use your thumb to hold the thread in place for each successive link. Keep the stitches even in tension and in size. On the reverse side the chain stitch should look like an even row of backstitches. *Linear*

Detached Chain Stitch (Lazy Daisy Stitch)

Bring the thread up at the base of the petal, hold loop with thumb, and anchor it with a small stitch. This stitch can be made in a ring with the base of each stitch very close for a round flower or as a filling stitch if you scatter them at random.   *Linear & Decorative*

Petal Stitch

This stitch combines an outline stitch and a lazy daisy stitch worked simultaneously. Take one outline stitch, bring the needle back to the middle of the stitch, make a detached chain to one side, then continue with another stitch of outline and repeat. You can vary this by making the petals alternate from side to side. It is important that you bring the needle out, after making the detached chain at the base of the chain, in the centre of your outline stitch. Then, coming out of the same hole, make another outline stitch and repeat the chain.   *Linear*

Open Chain

This stitch, also called a "square chain," is just a plain chain that has been broadened. Instead of stitching into the same hole, be sure that your needle is placed a length away, diagonally. Do not pull your thread too tightly.   *Linear*

Zigzag Chain

This stitch is worked in the same manner as the open chain but the chains alternate from side to side.   *Linear*

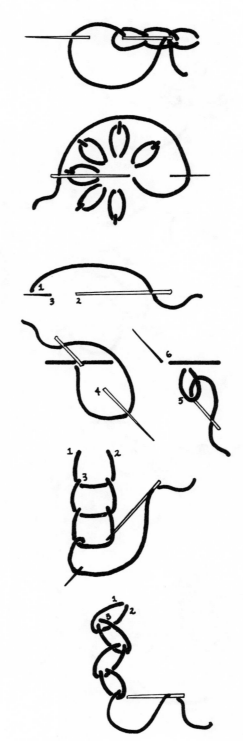

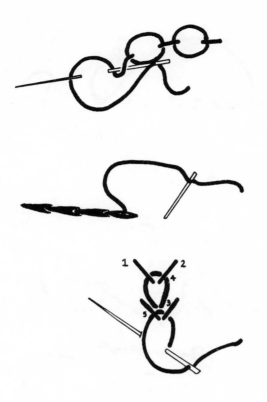

Cable Chain

As you bring the needle up and just before you make the second chain, twist your thread over and under the needle and then continue stitching. Some stitchers find it easier to learn this stitch by working from the top down. *Linear*

Split Stitch

Work this stitch the same way you would an outline stitch, but be sure to split your thread at the base of each stitch, creating a very fine chain-like stitch. *Decorative*

Wheatear Stitch

This stitch starts with two small stitches forming an angle, taken top to bottom. Next form a chain loop without entering the fabric by passing the thread *behind* the angle. Connect each chain by repeating the process. This can also be used as a detached stitch. *Linear*

Knotted Stitches

Knotted stitches are easily identified by their studded appearance. They may be used singly or in a line, as fillings, open, or solid. They produce a rich, irregular surface that will contrast with the smooth flat stitches.

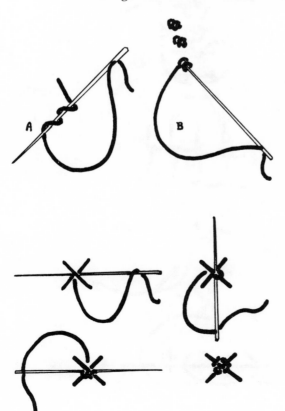

French Knot

Use a round-eyed needle so that the coil slips off easily. Bring the thread out at the required position, hold it down with the left thumb and wind the thread twice or even three times around the needle. It is best to let the point of the needle encircle the thread (A). Still keeping the thread taut, revolve the needle around until the point of it is close to where the thread first came through. Insert the needle and thread through to the back of the material (B). If properly made the knot will resemble a bead laid endways up upon the material. *Linear & Decorative*

Spanish Knots

Begin this with a cross-stitch. Next, using the backstitch movement, insert the needle behind the cross horizontally. Continue this sequence until all legs of the cross-stitch are looped. The final backstitch is carried through to the back of the fabric. *Decorative*

Bullion Knot

Pick up a backstitch the size of the bullion stitch required and bring the needle point out where it first emerged. Do *not* pull the needle right through the fabric. Wind the thread around the needle point as many times as is necessary (A) to equal the space of the backstitch. With your left thumb, hold the coiled thread and pull the needle through. Still holding the coiled thread, turn the needle back to where it was inserted and insert in the same place (B). Pull the thread through until the bullion stitch lies flat. A needle with a small, round eye works best as it then allows the thread to pass through the coils more easily. *Linear & Decorative*

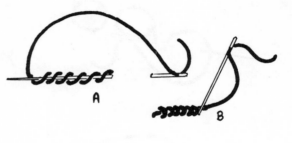

Coral Stitch

This stitch makes a somewhat irregular but decorative line. Bring the thread through at the right end of a line. Hold the thread down upon the material along the line to be worked. Insert the needle and pull it through. The thread is passed under the needle. *Linear*

Detached Stitches

This group consists of those stitches, as the name implies, that are detached from the ground material while being worked. They are attached to the surface stitches only and mostly used for bold borders, fillers of large areas, or to cover raw edges in crazy patchwork.

Raised Chain Band

Place foundation threads about 1/8" (0.3 cm) apart. Work chain stitch over each of the bars. *Linear*

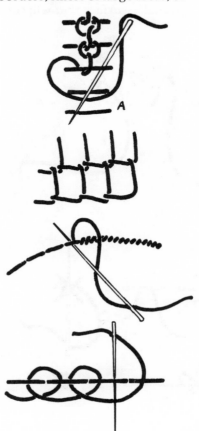

Detached Buttonhole Stitch

This stitch is worked from left to right and back again. Work one row of buttonhole stitch. Then work back again, working only on the threads, not on the material. *Linear*

Overcast Backstitch

Work a backstitch and then with a thinner thread working from left to right, overcast it. *Linear*

Pekinese Stitch

Work a row of backstitch. Then interlace with matching or contrasting thread as shown in the diagram. Keep the loops the same size. *Linear*

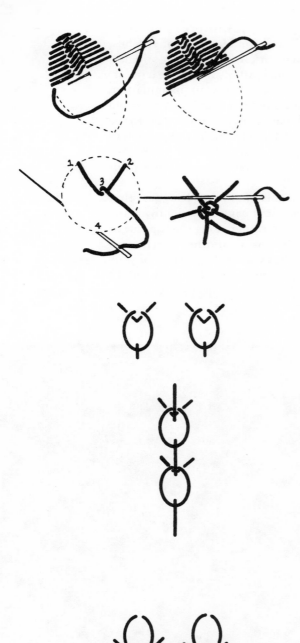

Romanian Stitch

Bring the thread through at the bottom left of the shape to be filled, carry the thread across, and take a stitch on the right side of the shape with the thread below the needle. Take a stitch at the left side, thread above the needle. Alternate these two movements until the shape is filled. Keep the stitches close together.   *Linear & Decorative*

Spider's Web Filling (woven)

Make a fly stitch in the centre of the circle. Work two straight stitches, one on each side of the fly stitch tail into the centre of the circle so that it is divided into five equal sections. Weave over and under the "spokes" until the circle is filled.   *Decorative*

Tête de Boeuf Stitch

The name of this stitch means literally "ox head" which it resembles. First work a detached fly stitch to form the horns. Instead of a plain anchoring stitch, the fly stitch is held down by a detached chain as shown in the diagram.   *Decorative*

Chain and Fly Stitch

This stitch looks very much like the wheatear stitch and the slipped detached chain but is worked quite differently. Begin with a tête de boeuf stitch and as the chain is anchored, bring your needle out to the side, ready to begin the next fly stitch. (The texture of each of the three stitches varies somewhat, although their appearance is similar.)   *Linear & Decorative*

Chain Stitch, Slipped

This stitch is often called the *tulip stitch* because that is what it looks like. When working it, first work a fairly large detached chain stitch. When completing the tie stitch, bring the needle out again as if making a fly stitch attached to the bottom of the detached chain. Then "slip" the needle under the tie stitch and take it into the fabric. More than one "slipped" stitch can be added to enrich the stitch. Think about using a second or third color for the "slipped" stitches.   *Decorative*

Stitch Combinations and Variations

Much of the pleasure in working the stitches of crazy patchwork comes from the selection of stitches, variations of stitches, and combinations of stitches. Initially, you may work most of your crazy patchwork using the basic stitches, but soon the fascination of creating your own combinations will prove irresistable. The pages of combinations given here may spark your imagination. I made them from an accumulation of notes and sketches that I took from old patchwork quilts as well as from choosing two basic stitches and trying to see how many different combinations I could derive from them. You may wish to keep a small notebook in your workbag and record your own inspired stitches as soon as they come to you. I know from experience that if the stitches are not recorded *instantly* they are gone forever.

If you are eager to make your own combinations of stitches I suggest that you check the Combination Stitch Chart on the next page and see how many different stitches you can produce by running your finger along the top row of the boxes of stitches, selecting one, and then choosing another stitch from those along the side. Your combinations of stitches will be the product of your own imagination. Many varieties of stitches are combined in Dorothy Bond's books and L. R. Hen's *Needlework Designs from Old Crazy Quilts* (see Reference Reading, page 20).

TIPS   How To Vary Simple Stitches

All stitches can be varied, depending on
• how close together the stitches are,
• the angle of the needle going into the material,
• the length of the stitches,
• the sequence of the length of the stitches and whether the stitches are joined or detached,
• the direction of the stitches (work stitches backwards, forwards, up, down, sideways, slanted, etc., to make them look different),
• the thickness or thinness of the thread or yarn,
• the use of the same color or contrasting color thread to whip or lace the stitches, and
• the position of one row of stitching worked atop another row for interesting texture.

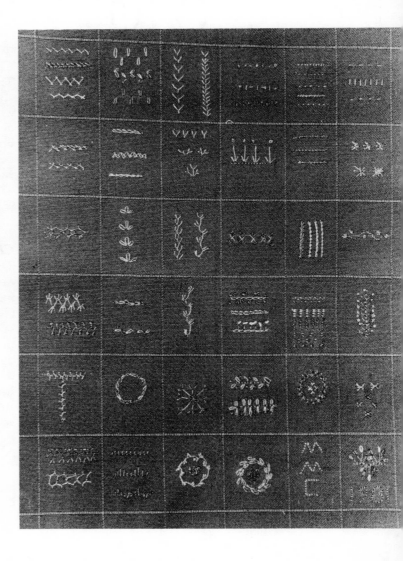

Combination Stitch Chart

Basic Stitch: Herringbone	Basic Stitch: Lazy Daisy	Basic Stitch: Fly Stitch	Basic Stitch: French Knot	Basic Stitch: Stem Stitch / Running Stitch	Basic Stitch: Straight Stitch
Threaded Herringbone Use two colors of thread for best effect.	Chain Stitch	Single Featherstitch	French Knots with Straight Stitches	Laced Running Stitch Use two colors for best effect.	Star Stitch
Herringbone with Straight Stitches	Triple Lazy Daisy	Double Featherstitch	French Knots with Cross–Stitch	Couching Two colors are best	Star Stitch to decorate seam with Stem Stitch
Closed Herringbone	Lazy Daisies with French Knots	Triple Featherstitch	French Knots and Scroll Stitch	Couching — Two colors laid down with a third color	Straight Stitch with French Knots
Closed Herringbone with Tied Stitches Use a second color for tying stitches	Chain Stitch, Stem, and Fly Stitches	Fly Stitch with Straight Stitch	Lazy Daisy with French Knots	Running Stitch Parallel rows of multicolor	Straight Stitches — "wheat" effect
Blanket Stitch	Herringbone (double) and Chain Stitch	Two variations of Fly Stitches	French Knots Stem Stitch Lazy Daisy	Stem Stitch (meandering) with Straight Stitches and French Knots	Straight Stitch and French Knots

Chain Stitch
Combinations and Variations

Chain Stitches "C"

C I with detached vertical chain stitches

C II with vertical flat stitches

C III Vertical chain with horizontal detached chain and horizontal flat stitch

C IV Vertical chain with detached horizontal chains

C V Triple chains

C VI Zigzag chain stitch with detached chain and french knots

C VII Star stitch with detached chain and french knots

C VIII Detached chain flowers along the seamline plus double detached chain leaves (work in 2 colors)

C IX Triple detached chain with large french knots

C X Stem — backstitch
Leaves — detached chain
Flower — closed fly stitch

C XI Five detached chains in petal shape

C XII Meandering stem with detached chain

C XIII Detached chains forming flower shape: stem stitch and detached chain

C XIV Large and small chains alternated

C XV Chains in roundel

C XVI Chain — oval with detached chain

C XVII Detached chain and flat stitches

C XVIII Triple detached chains

C XIX Petal stitch with "slipped" stitch and flat stitch in centre

C XX Petal stitch
Backstitch
French knots

C XXI Triple detached chains

Knotted Stitch Combinations and Variations

Knotted Stitches "KS"

KS I Squared palestrina knot

KS II Bullion knots in leaf shape and flat stitch

KS III Bullion knots in roundel Detached chains in centre

KS IV Bullion spray
Stem stitch, 5 bullion knots per spray, fly stitch, and flat stitch

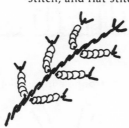

Blanket (Buttonhole) Stitch Combinations and Variations

Blanket Stitches "B"

B I Double blanket stitch with detached chains

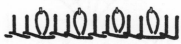

B II Alternating double blanket stitch

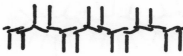

B III Blanket stitch with triple detached chain

B IV Double reversed blanket stitch — french knots, and detached chains

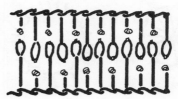

B V Closed buttonhole — reversed

B VI Buttonhole with french knots

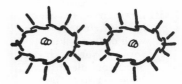

B VII Buttonhole and reverse buttonhole

B VIII Straight stitch, detached chains, running stitch

B IX Graduated blanket stitch worked in elliptical shapes

B X Closed buttonhole and closed buttonhole reversed

B XI Buttonhole worked in roundel

B XII Buttonhole in cross shape, cross-stitch in centre

B XIII Draw circle: Divide in half horizontally, then with diagonal lines as shown. Work each group of buttonhole stitches from a central point.

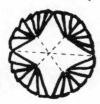

B XIV Crossed buttonhole
Open   Closed

B XV Groups of buttonhole with "scalloped" edging

B XVI Alternating open and closed buttonhole

B XVII Diagonal buttonhole and closed buttonhole

B XVIII Closed buttonhole

B XIX Graduating buttonhole

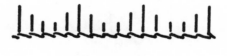

B XX Buttonhole in roundel

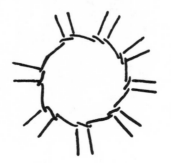

Fly Stitch Combinations and Variations

Fly Stitches "Fly"

Fly I Star stitch and detached fly stitches

Fly II Attached fly stitch in star shape

Fly III Attached fly stitches with french knots
Bow — two small and two large detached chain
Heart — satin stitch

Fly IV Open cretan stitch plus detached fly stitch with large french knots

Fly V Closed horizontal fly stitch and reversed plus french knots

CS VII Cross-stitch arranged in a triangle with straight stitches

CS VIII Cross-stitches arranged in squares

CS IX Cross-stitch flower Two cross-stitches worked on top of each other with the second stitch being interwoven with the first

CS X Cross-stitches in roundel

Herringbone Stitch Combinations and Variations

Herringbone Stitches "H"

H I Herringbone with fly stitch and straight stitch

H II Herringbone with triple detached chains

H III Double herringbone reversed

H IV Herringbone — tied with detached chains

H V Double herringbone reversed with detached fly stitches

H VI Herringbone with french knots

H VII Herringbone with alternating tied stitches and vertical straight stitch

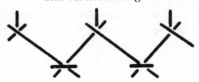

H VIII Herringbone stitch with five straight stitches held down by a small stitch in contrasting color

H IX Herringbone plus french knots alternating with upright crosses

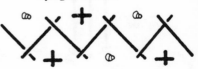

H X Herringbone and flat stitches

H XI Threaded herringbone

Flat Stitch
Combinations and Variations

Flat Stitches "FS"

FS I Star stitch with running stitch

FS II Fly stitch, flat stitch, running stitch, french knots

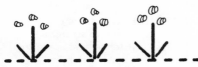

FS III Flat stitch, fly stitch, and french knot

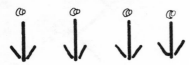

FS IV Three flat stitches and french knots

FS V Cross-stitch with horizontal flat stitch

FS VI Star stitch arranged in triangle

FS VII Flat stitch and star stitch

FS VIII Diagonal flat stitch and star stitch

FS IX Straight and diagonal flat stitches

FS X Flat stitch with french knot and cross-stitch

FS XI Flat stitches radiating from a french knot

FS XII Fan shaped flat stitch and french knot

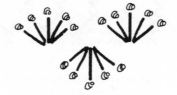

FS XIII Wheat stitch

FS XIV Fly stitch and flat stitches arranged in fan shapes

FS XV Fern stitch

FS XVI Flat stitch arranged in fan shape

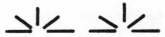

Tools

The items listed below will not be repeated for each project. For additional details about construction techniques please refer to Judy Brittain (ed.), *The Bantom Step-by-Step Book of Needlecraft* (Bantom Books Inc., Toronto, 1979) and Sally Read (ed.), *The Needleworker's Constant Companion* (Viking Press, New York, 1978).

Sewing bag
Yard or metre stick
Embroidery hoops
Imperial or metric tape measure
Dressmaker's tracing paper
Clear plastic ziplock bags
Sharp HB lead pencil
Sharp artist's white pencil
Water-soluble marking pens
Clip-on magnifiers
Sharp scissors
Small pair needle-nosed pliers
Selection of sewing and embroidery needles in different sizes (see page 18)
Glass-headed long dressmaker's pins, pin cushion
Seam ripper
Tweezers
Thimble
White and light-colored thread for basting
Iron and ironing board
Press cloth
Onionskin paper for tracing designs from book
Trace-a-Pattern™, Do-Sew™ or inexpensive white tissue paper and cellophane tape for "scaling up" graphed patterns
Sewing machine, preferably with decorative stitches or cams and zigzag stitch
Thumbtacks or thick pins to pin tissue paper to cutting board
Folding cardboard cutting board

Terms and Definitions

Batts   Commercially made padding for quilts and quilted items.

Bonded quilt batting   This is a commercial quilt batt that has a chemical coating to keep it from falling apart when washed. It gives a slightly stiff feel to the surface of your quilting — the cheaper the batt, the more pronounced the stiffness. Use cheaper batts for flat items where body is needed. For clothing, buy the best quality bonded batting you can find so that it will mold to the body and drape nicely.

Comforter batt   Commercially made padding for comforters, extra thick.

Do-Sew™   Brand name for a type of nonwoven transparent material for drafting patterns and making pattern adjustments. It can be sewn by hand or machine and is quite durable.

Double needle   This has one shank but two needles and can be substituted for the ordinary needle on most sewing machines. It sews an even line of double stitching on the top but the underside is one wavy line of stitching. It is best used where the underside does not show.

Echo quilting   This quilting follows the line of the applique piece so that the shape of the quilting "echoes" the shape of the applique. It is usually used when more than one line of quilting is required. The lines are about 1/4" (0.6 cm) apart.

Embellish   This means to decorate the surface of the item using threads and/or other decorative items such as beads, sequins, applied ribbons, etc., including painting with fibre paints.

Embroider   Such instruction means to decorate the surface of the item with a variety of decorative stitches.

Fabric gluestick   This is a type of solid glue developed for use on fabrics. It is in the form of a swivel-up stick and does not usually stain materials. As a precaution, however, test some on the materials you plan to use before using it on your project.

Fusible interfacing   This is a nonwoven material with an adhesive on one side that is activated by heat (from an iron) and moisture (from your steam iron and/or wet press cloth). Check the manufacturers' directions and follow carefully for best results. This material comes in light-, medium-, and heavy-weights. Be sure to choose the correct interfacing weight for the weight of the material you are using.

Ladder stitch   This is a type of construction (open chain stitch with corner knots) used in the making of boxes, frames, and some other projects.

Machine basting   Set your machine to the longest stitch length and do not backstitch at the ends.

Machine embroidery thread   This finer thread has more sheen to it than ordinary sewing thread. It is made especially for embroidering by machine. Often, it comes on larger spools and/or cones than ordinary sewing thread.

Overlapping   Such instructions mean to position a lighter piece of material over a heavier piece so that prominent ridges are avoided when making crazy patchwork.

Pearl cotton   This is a type of twisted, cotton embroidery thread that comes in a wide range of colors and three diameters — the finest is #8, medium is #5, and the coarsest is #3. Most projects in this book call for #8.

Pin baste   Such instruction means to use small gold safety pins to baste (hold together) layers of fabric rather than using needle and thread.

Polyfil   This is a trade name for a type of unbonded batting that is made especially for stuffing pillows and toys.

Pressor foot   The foot on your sewing machine that presses the fabric against the feed dogs which move the fabric along when the pressor bar is lowered.

Quilting "in-the-ditch"   Such instructions refer to quilting down the groove of the seam from the front so that the quilting is virtually invisible. This procedure may be done by hand or machine.

Stranded embroidery cotton   This is embroidery thread that is supplied in one strand made up of six smaller strands that may be separated out to use for finer embroidery. Unless care is taken when working, this cotton may leave little loops of single threads.

Trace-a-Pattern™   This is a type of nonwoven transparent material, sometimes printed with red dots at 1" (2.5 cm) intervals for the purpose of drafting patterns and making pattern adjustments. This sewing aid is usually available in sewing supply stores or through the mail order sources given in this book (see page 176).

Unbonded quilt batting   This commercial batt has no chemical coating on it and may pull apart with laundering and/or wear. It is suitable for stuffing toys and pillows.

Pattern Making

Almost every quilter I know hates to enlarge graphed designs. However, space considerations in almost every publication make it imperative that one learn to do it. It is really very simple and requires absolutely *no talent for art or drawing!* These simple directions will take the mystery out of scaling up graphed designs.

The most important aid to enlarging designs is a folding cardboard cutting board available very reasonably in every sewing supply shop. Dritz™makes an excellent one marked both in imperial markings and metric. It takes very little space to store and you will soon learn to use it for every sewing project. Not only is it an aid in designing and scaling up designs but it makes a super surface on which to cut and it protects your table as well. It has useful aids printed on it such as curves, scallops, etc.

The next most useful sewing notion is Trace-a-Pattern™ or Do-Sew™. Both of these are nonwoven transparent materials that are sold by the yard or metre in your local sewing shop. I prefer the Trace-a-Pattern™ type that has dots (usually red) at 1″ (2.5 cm) intervals. The advantages to using this is that it can be pinned to your cutting board and lined up with the squares or pinned to the blank side. It can be machine basted so that you can try on the garment or partially make it up to be sure your pattern is correct. It can be slashed and taped smaller or pieces can be put in using cellophane tape to make it larger. The pattern can then be tried on again. Once the pattern is created, it is reuseable indefinitely.

If this sewing aid is unavailable in your area, tissue paper (white, cheapest you can find) will work but it does not drape as well. In addition, you may have to draw the appropriate size squares on the paper before scaling up the pattern. An alternative is to pin the paper, taped together to get the right size, to the side of the cutting board that is measured off.

With the scaled diagram in front of you, simply count off the squares at the widest and longest part and with a ballpoint pen and a long ruler, draw along the large graph marks. Then, square by square, draw in what you see in each square. Throughout the project directions the scale is given on each piece, as it varies occasionally depending on the size of the project. For example, the scale is that each small square on the diagram given for the St. Clare of Assisi wall panel is equal to 2″ (5 cm) on your full-size pattern. However, on the "stained-glass" vest pattern the scale is one square on the diagram equals 1″ (2.5 cm) on the scaled-up full-size pattern you are creating. The sketches usually indicate if seam allowance has been included. However, as a precaution include a 1/2″ (1.25 cm) seam allowance on each piece.

This is a sample of Trace-a-Pattern™ with red dots.

Changing Pattern Size

Pattern sizes are given in medium but they can be made smaller or larger. As a general rule, there is about 2″ (5 cm) difference between the measurements for each size. Therefore, when making the "try-on" pattern (in Trace-a-Pattern™ so that you can make adjustments on the mock-up) if the sketch is given for a *medium size* and you need a *large size* add at least 2″ (5 cm). To be absolutely sure, take your bust, upper bust, and hip measurements, plus bodice length and skirt length, and compare them against those given in the pattern.

Remember to divide the total number of inches you need to add (or subtract) by four (the number of pattern edges you have) and add or subtract that figure from each pattern piece edge. Keep in mind that patterns already have "pattern ease" built in so that they are not skin-tight.

If you are nervous about making patterns, you can purchase a commercial pattern in your size and adapt it to the project. However, it would be well worth your time and the price of some inexpensive material to try making your own pattern. Jean Ray Laury, a noted American quilt authority, in a workshop she taught and which I attended in Ithaca, N.Y. in 1976 said, "Give yourself a present of several yards of inexpensive material and play with it, trying out new techniques. If you ruin it, you've still had fun and learned something." If you can't bring yourself to use new material, keep your worn-out sheets for making mock-up patterns.

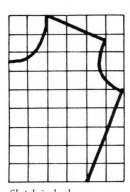

Sketch in book
1 square = 1/2″ (1.25 cm)

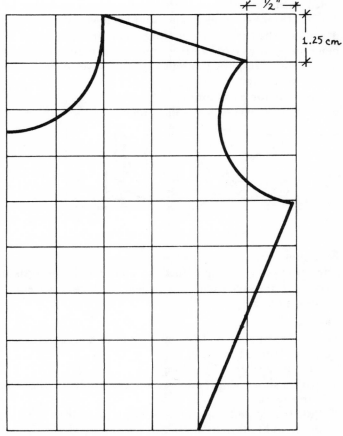

Scaled-up design

Decorative Facings

Decorative facings, worked with crazy patchwork, can be added to any neckline. Diagram A shows how to trace the shape of the neckline from the main pattern piece and extend it so that you can shape it. Diagram B shows the facing assembled with the raw outer edge turned under or else finished in some other neat manner. Diagram C shows the method of attaching the facing to the garment neckline and Diagram D shows how to attach the outer edge to the shoulder seam so that it does not shift.

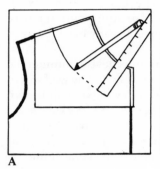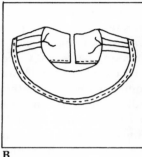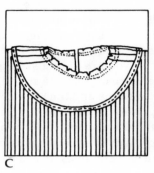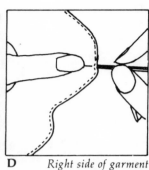

A   B   C   D   *Right side of garment and decorative facing*

Piping

Keep the following points in mind when you are using piping.

1. Purchase sufficient cable cord (in the diameter you want) to go around your project and add a little — 1/4 yd (22.5 cm) — for insurance.
2. Cut a bias binding of fabric wide enough to cover the cable cord including 1/2" (1.25 cm) seam allowances on both sides.
3. Enclose the cord in the binding and with the zipper foot attachment on your machine, sew as close to the edge of the piping as possible.
4. When applying the piping to another layer of material, stitch it *over* the first line of stitching.
5. Apply as for bias binding.
6. Trim away excess seam allowance.

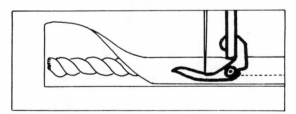

Fringes

Fringes make a striking finish to some of the designs in this book. General directions are given with the projects but here are complete instructions for making a fringe.

Method 1

1. Wind yarn four or five times around a cardboard strip cut the depth you want the fringe to be (A).
2. Cut the bottom of the loops.
3. With a sharp object such as a dressmaker's awl or a crochet hook, make a hole in the item.
4. Pull the folded edge of the loops (top) through this, pass the cut ends through and pull tightly (B).

Method 2 Self-Fringe

1. Machine stitch a row of stay-stitching across the fabric at the top edge of where you want the fringe to be (A).

2. Carefully, with a tapestry needle which has a blunt edge, remove one thread at a time until you work up to the stay-stitching (B). It is a good idea to run a double row of stay-stitching. Method 2 will not work on very tightly woven material.

Method 1

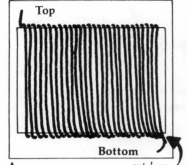

A   *cut here*   B

Method 2

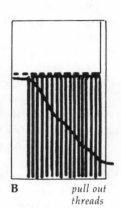

A   B   *pull out threads*

Ruffles

Ruffles are attractive and can often add a feminine or soft finish to garments and pillows.

1. Calculate the amount of fabric required to give the desired fullness (twice the measurement of the edge for a full effect or one and a half times the measurement of the edge for a less full effect). Cut this length and join the raw ends; press.

2. Make a row of running stitches about 1/8″ (0.3 cm) just inside the seam allowance of the edge to be gathered. Use the longest straight stitch on your sewing machine (A). To avoid having your thread break while gathering, do the stitching in four separate sections. Then if the thread breaks you have only to re-do part of the work! These sections can also guide you in evening up the gathers.

3. Pin the ruffle at section points to the item edge (also divided into four).

4. Loosen or tighten the row of gathers to get the gathers even.

5. With right sides together, pin edges. Place pins at right angles to the edge so that you can machine sew over them.

6. Wind the thread ends around a pin as illustrated so that they don't pull out while you are adjusting the other areas (B).

7. Machine stitch along the seamline with the gathered side up to avoid bunching or flattening the ruffle (C). Remove gathering threads.

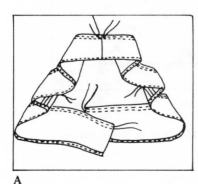

A

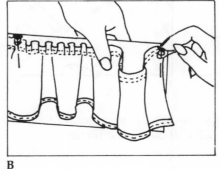

B

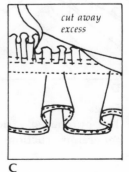

cut away excess

C

Garment Closures

There are several ways to fasten a finished garment. Here are some choices and directions for closures.

Open
Leave the garment with no fastening (see the San Diego Spring jacket project).

Ties
These are perfect for children's garments and add interest to women's garments, too. But they are usually too feminine in appearance for a man's item.

1. Cut a strip 12" x 1-3/4" (30 cm x 4.4 cm) for each tie.
2. Fold strip in half with right sides together, stitching on the machine with a 1/8" (0.3 cm) seam.
3. Turn right side out. Press.
4. Baste one short end of each strip in place along the front edge. This permits ties to be secured when garment edge is bound. Slip stitch raw end closed (A).
5. Apply binding over the edge.

Fabric Loops

1. Make as directed for ties.
2. Cut each strip into pieces 2-1/2" long (6.25 cm).
3. You can press into a mitred loop as shown in diagram (B) and proceed as above, or
4. You can make plain loops (C), pin in place (D), and proceed as before (E) (F).

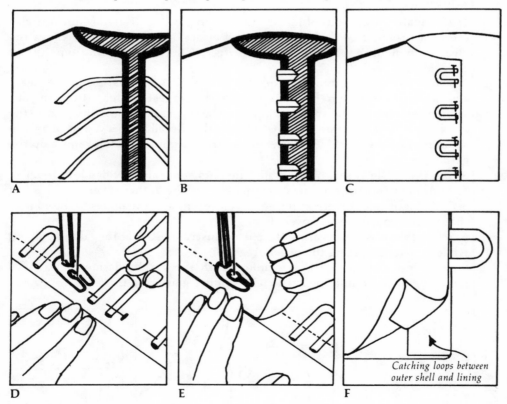

Catching loops between outer shell and lining

Frogs
The purchased variety are best. If you choose to make them, any book on general instructions will give detailed directions.

Prairie Point Buttonholes
This is my favorite closure. If you make a mistake, you can simply re-do the prairie point!

1. Make the required number of prairie points, using the second method as shown on page 60. Steam press.
2. Most garments look better with an odd number of loops or points.
3. Open up the folds at the centre and work the buttonhole by hand or machine (A).
4. Attach as for loops.
5. Raw edges will be covered by binding or concealed in the seam edges.

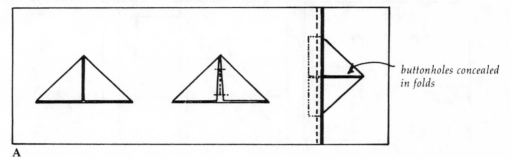

buttonholes concealed in folds

A

Crocheted Loop and Fancy Buttons
Choose buttons suitable for the garment and crochet a loop of the proper size.

Closures should be placed at the neck, fullest part of the bust or chest, and waist. Space the others in between.

Note: The most important thing to remember about choosing a closure is that the type chosen should be compatible with the style and feeling of the garment, (i.e.) sporty, feminine, masculine, dressy, etc.

Mitred Corners

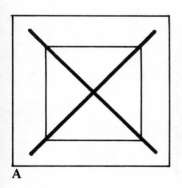

A

A mitre board can be helpful in the tricky business of mitring corners. Prepare a piece of soft board 14" x 8" (35 cm x 20 cm) by wrapping it in several thicknesses of muslin or flannelette. Staple or thumbtack the material in place. On the board, using a T-square and doing it first in pencil, duplicate the markings as shown on the diagram. Make two or three size variations. On my board I have a 2" (5 cm) square, a 4" (10 cm) square, and a 6" (15 cm) square. These are the sizes I use most often. When you are satisfied that the markings are accurate and straight, go over them with indelible ballpoint pen. *Do not use a felt tip marker. Using the steam iron may cause it to run into your binding.*

Using the Mitre Board
1. Pin the two strips of binding in place over the board. Mark with pencil.
2. Pin your seam along the diagonal marking and baste if you wish.
3. Machine sew along the diagonal mark.
4. Check to be sure that the corner is a 45° angle and then trim the excess material.

Mitring with Binding
This procedure presents some difficulty for many people so I am giving more than one method. I recommend that you cut a piece of prequilted material about 12" (30 cm) square and about 4" (10 cm) of binding and practise these methods. You can then select the method you like best.

Method 1

1. Leave an amount equal to the width of the binding plus seam allowance extending on both sides of the corners (A).
2. Fold the item on the diagonal. The right side of your item should be out. The *wrong side* of the binding will be towards you (B). Pin well.
3. Fold both pieces of border down to form a 90° angle. Be sure to leave 1/2" (1.25 cm) seam allowance. Pin well.
4. Insert scissors into the fold and cut both borders from X to Y (C).
5. Discard the pieces you cut off; pin ends of border and machine stitch.

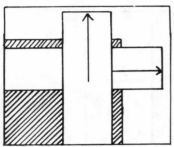 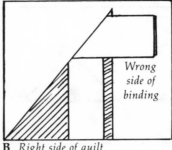 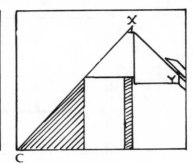

A *Right side of quilt*   B *Right side of quilt*   C

Method 2

1. Begin to sew the binding along one side of the fabric towards a corner. Stop stitching the width of your seam allowance from the corner. Cut thread and fasten ends (A).
2. After folding the binding to bring it around the corner, start stitching again on the very edge of the fabric (B).
3. Clip the corner of the material and turn the binding to the wrong side.
4. Form the mitre at the corner. Whipstitch (C).
5. Stitch the binding in place on the wrong side.

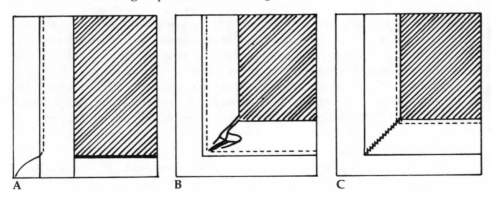

A   B   C

How to attach binding to the back of the article (diagram on page 53)
1. Pin the binding in place until just before the corner. Pin on the diagonal so that the corner is securely held (A).
2. Pick up the ends of the binding that are sticking up and trim them off being sure to leave about 1/2" (1.25 cm) to tuck into the hem (B) (C).
3. Fold one raw edge over the other and pin (D).
4. With matching thread and a fine close whipstitch, close the corner (E).

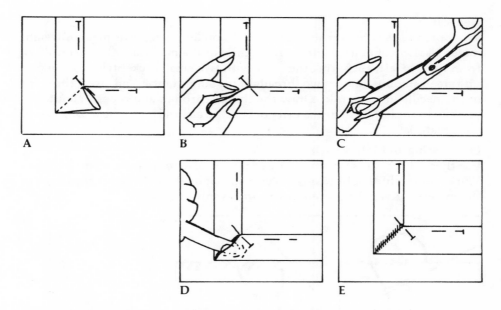

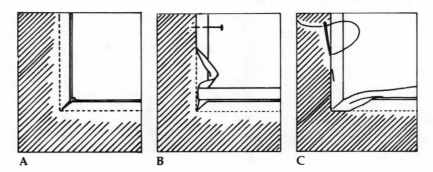

Mitring Inside Corners

You can use either double-fold or single-fold bias binding to do this.

1. Stitch to the width of the seam allowance beyond the cut corner of the fabric.
2. Pivot the fabric on the needle to turn the corner and continue stitching down the seamline (A).
3. Clip the seam and corner.
4. Turn the binding to the wrong side (B) and stitch in place by hand (C).

Hand Stitching

Basting

This stitch is used to hold the fabric together temporarily. I use white basting thread on dark items and put the knot on the top where it can easily be removed. If you are basting white or light-colored items, *do not use* a very dark thread. It may be easy to see but it tends to leave the color in the needle holes. Instead, use a light but contrasting thread. Make even but fairly long stitches (1/4" to 1/2" or 0.6 cm to 1.25 cm) (A). If you have to ease one of the fabrics, place it on top and gently gather it as you work.

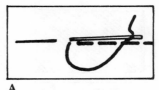

Hemstitch

This stitch is used for turning under hems on lightweight or mediumweight materials. Do not pull the thread too tightly or the material will pucker. Work from right to left, anchoring the work with two small backstitches. Then pick up a small amount, one or two threads of the single fabric, and insert the point of the needle into the fold. Draw the thread through and repeat, about 1/4" (0.6 cm) to the left (B). The majority of your thread will be on the wrong side of your material.

Overcasting and Whipstitch

Use these stitches for finishing raw edges and also for joining seams by hand. Work from right to left, taking very small diagonal stitches over the edges of the material. Keep them even in size and evenly spaced (C).

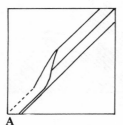
B

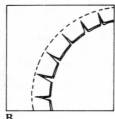
C

Types of Seams

Basic Seam

This is a flat seam used to join two pieces of fabric. Usually plain, straight stitches are used on a basic seam (A).

Plain Curved Seams

These seams can be used to join curved pieces. It is important to stay-stitch just outside the seamlines on both edges so that the fabric does not stretch. Sew with the concave edge uppermost and machine stitch on the seamline so that the stay-stitching does not show. Cut notches out of the seam allowance to take out any extra fullness (B). Press the seam with the tip of the iron only (C).

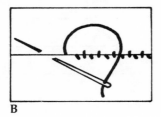
A

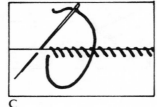
B

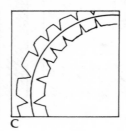
C

French Seam

This seam is really a seam within another seam. Place the wrong sides of the fabric together and take a small, 1/4" (0.6 cm) seam (A). Press for best results. Trim seam (if necessary) and then with right sides of the fabric together, fold on the stitch line and pin well. Machine stitch along the seam allowance (B). This makes a reversible seam and it is very strong.

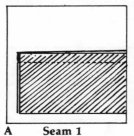
A   Seam 1

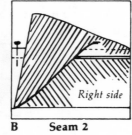
B   Seam 2

Right side

Flat Felled Seam

This seam is used for most sports clothes and reversible fabrics, especially if the material is bulky. Sew a straight seam, right sides together (A). Trim the under seam allowance close to the stitching line. Then turn under the raw edge of the upper seam allowance and pin and stitch down by hand or machine (B).

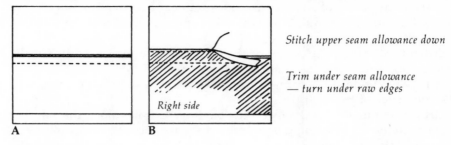

Stitch upper seam allowance down

Trim under seam allowance — turn under raw edges

Seam Finishing

Pinking   Trim the seam allowance using pinking shears (A).

Zigzag Stitching by Machine   This is used to finish seams that will otherwise fray. Use the zigzag stitch on the sewing machine (B).

Overcasting   This is used if you do not have a zigzag sewing machine (C).

Crossed Seam   This is used when two specially finished seams cross. Finish off the seams before sewing the two pieces together. Making the seams match up is important so put a straight pin into the stitching line where they will cross before you stitch. Stitch the seam carefully, making sure that the material does not shift. To reduce bulk, after stitching, trim the seam allowance on the diagonal as shown in the sketch (D).

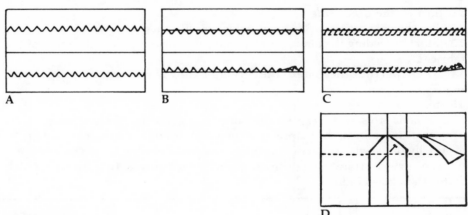

Binding

You can use either a straight-edge binding or a bias binding. For many edge finishes, where there are few or only gentle curves, it is possible to use straight binding. This is the fastest to make and it is easy to apply. Double-thickness binding wears better and should always be used.

Straight-Edge Binding

1. Cut the binding the required width across the width of the fabric if possible.
2. Join lengths until you have the required length of binding that you need (A).
3. Press in half and attach (B).

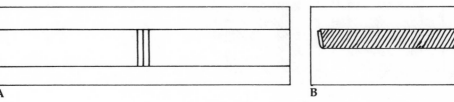

Applying Straight-Edge Binding

1. Cut the fabric on the straight grain, 1-1/2" (3.8 cm) and put several pieces together so it is long enough to go around the perimeter of whatever it is you are binding (measure the perimeter of the item and add 2" or 5 cm for each corner to be turned).

2. Start in the centre of any straight side (not near a corner or point). Leave about 6" (15 cm) free so you can join the other end to it. Do not pin the binding to the quilt; it is not necessary.

3. Stitch to within 1/4" (0.6 cm) of the corner, fasten off your stitching by backstitching, and *remove from machine* (A).

4. Pin the next side at the corner through the binding only and parallel with the second edge of the quilt (B).

5. Lift this pin up (it is still only on the binding) so it lies along the side you have just stitched. The binding now forms a square corner on the quilt.

6. Remove the pin, holding the corner in place with your hand, and pin the mitre in place. This will leave a tuck at the corner that is essential to the process.

7. Start machine sewing again, using the same seam allowance you used before but starting right at the edge of the quilt.

8. Repeat these steps at each corner.

9. When you are within 6" (15 cm) of where you started, remove the quilt from the machine, pin the raw edges of the binding to the quilt, and find the point where you will join the binding together (C).

10. Sew with machine and press.

11. Put quilt back under the machine and finish sewing the binding to the quilt.

To turn to the other side

12. Pin the corners first. This may take a bit of practise.

13. Start by folding the binding on one side of a corner to the full extent of the fabric (D).

14. Then fold the other side of the corner binding to meet the machine stitching (E).

15. Sew down.

Note: Practise this on a scrap of fabric until you get it right before using it on a project. It is well worth the practice time and can be used on many projects, especially those with square corners and square armholes. If a garment edge is not too curved, straight-edge binding can be used successfully and it is much faster than bias binding.

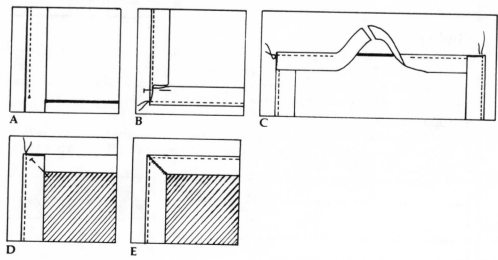

Bias

Once you have made your own bias binding you will never buy commercial binding again! Follow these simple steps and you'll see how easy it is.

1. Cut a square of any size. Refer to the chart on page 58 for the size of square necessary to make any yardage of binding.
2. Press the square in half diagonally and cut accurately on this fold (A).
3. Assemble so that it looks like diagram (B), (i.e.) be sure that the straight edges of the triangle are together. Machine stitch with a fine stitch.
4. Press the seam open and then open the material up so that it looks like diagram (C).
5. Measure off the width (remember you need double the width of the finished binding) across the parallelogram. Do this very accurately (C). Useful measuring devices are the plastic strips available for cutting seminole patch-work strips. You can purchase these in different widths.
6. Reassemble into a tube shape as shown but offset the strips by one so that a "tag" sticks up at the top and one at the bottom (D). (Otherwise, when you cut along the marked lines, you get little doughnut shapes!)
7. Pin the two diagonal sides together very carefully so that the offset lines match up accurately *at the seamline.* Lay the material down to check.
8. Machine stitch the pinned sides with a fine stitch. Check to be sure that your seam will be on the same side as your previous seam!
9. Take to your ironing board and press the seam open. You will have a tube shape.
10. Still at the board, slip the strip over the end and cut along the marked lines.
11. Press in half and roll around a tube of cardboard until ready for use.

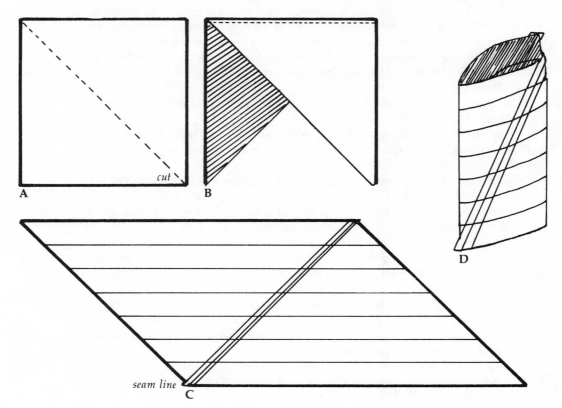

Yardage Chart For Bias Stripping

Read the chart either from left or right — from the left if you want to know how much stripping a certain amount of material will give, from the right if you know how much stripping you need and want to know the size of the square to start with.

All seam allowances are 1/4" (0.6 cm)

Size of square		Width of cut stripping		Width of folded stripping		Finished width of stripping — 1 side		Yards of stripping	
36"	90 cm	1.5"	3.75 cm	3/4"	1.9 cm	1/8"	0.3 cm	24"	60 cm
36"	90 cm	2"	5 cm	1.8"	4.5 cm	1/4"	0.6 cm	18"	45 cm
36"	90 cm	2.5"	6.25 cm	1.25"	3.12 cm	3/4"	1.9 cm	14.5"	36.25 cm
36"	90 cm	3"	7.5 cm	1.5"	3.75 cm	1"	2.5 cm	12"	30 cm
24"	60 cm	1.5"	3.75 cm	3/4"	1.9 cm	1/8"	0.3 cm	16"	40 cm
24"	60 cm	2"	5.00 cm	1.0"	2.5 cm	1/4"	0.6 cm	12"	30 cm
24"	60 cm	2.5"	6.25 cm	1.25"	3.12 cm	3/4"	1.9 cm	9.6"	24 cm
24"	60 cm	3"	7.5 cm	1.5"	3.75 cm	1"	2.5 cm	8"	20 cm

Pressing Bias Binding

This little trick was taught to me by one of my students, Beulah Hamilton of North Bay, Ontario who tells me it is one of the things taught by the Women's Institutes. There are numerous gadgets on the market to help you to make bias binding but this little notion will cost you nothing but a few moments of your time. It can be used to make single-fold bias with both edges turned under or to make double-fold bias, and you can make different sizes with it as well. Follow these simple steps.

1. Use a piece of board about 14" x 8" (35 cm x 20 cm) that is soft enough to put thumbtacks or staples into.

2. Wrap the board with several thicknesses of muslin, flannelette, or pre-quilted material and staple or thumbtack the material securely to the underside.

3. Cut a piece of stiff paper (from greeting cards is perfect) the width of the *finished* bias — the width of a yard or metre stick is good (about 1-1/8" wide or 2.8 cm). Remember to add 1/4" (0.6 cm) to each side of it for turning under. The final measurement will be 1-5/8" (approximately 4 cm).

4. Pin this paper to the top side of the bias board (A).

5. Make other strips using this method of calculation for other widths of bias that you commonly use; you can fit several on the board. Each paper should be the length of the sole plate of your iron.

6. I use double-fold bias most of the time so I have made a strip about 2" (5 cm) wide that includes the 1/4" plus 1/4" (0.6 cm plus 0.6 cm) seam allowance.

7. This is a two-step process — you will need a second "channel" to make the second fold. It is prepared in the same manner.

8. Using buttonhole or embroidery thread (doubled) in your needle, and a herringbone stitch (see diagram B) catch the material covering the board on each side of the length of the paper strip.

9. Remove the paper strip.

10. With the tip of your seam ripper or a small safety pin attached to the end of your bias strip, or a double length of thread caught at the end of the bias strip, thread the unfolded stripping through until it fills the space (C). *Note:* You will need to fold this first piece to the size you want it before threading.

11. Press with a steam iron (D).

12. Pull the end of the binding through; it will turn under automatically.

13. Press the next section and continue in this manner.

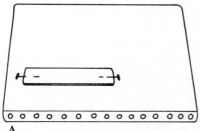

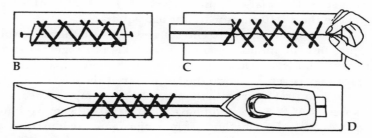

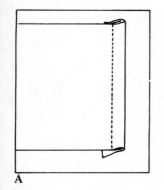

Applying Bias Binding

Bias bindings are neat, quickly made, and durable. A little practise will make you an expert in applying them. Here are some hints for binding application.

1. Baste or pin all loose edges of the garment down so they do not shift while you apply the binding.

2. Bindings may be applied to straight corners or curved corners. Straight binding is easier for square corners.

3. Whenever possible, round off a corner and apply the bias binding.

4. Start sewing on binding at a straight spot, *not at the corner.*

5. Use double-fold binding for good wear and appearance.

6. Sew the binding with raw edges of the binding and raw edges of the item together.

7. Start and stop securely.

8. Join raw ends of binding by hand.

9. Turn over and slipstitch the folded edge down by hand, OR

10. Machine "stitch-in-the-ditch" (A), with matching thread from the top. You will be able to feel the folded edge with your fingertips and so keep your stitching on this folded edge even though you can't see it.

11. When stitching in-the-ditch, it helps to pull a little more of the binding to the back so that you can catch it with your machine stitching.

12. Unless you are very expert this method will not be quite as attractive as doing it by hand but it will be strong and durable.

13. When binding an inside curve, stitch the bias binding on from the top side. Stretch the bias very taut so that it follows the curve.

Mock Bias Binding

If you have to make double bias binding that is quite large in scale, try using this method for a super neat job.

1. Cut a straight strip twice the width you want the finished binding to be.

2. With right sides together, stitch on machine (A).

3. Pull the material as you sew so it spirals (B).

4. Trim edges so they are straight.

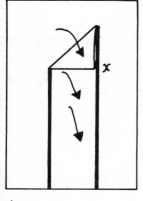

Place needle here and pull fabric to create a spiralling tube

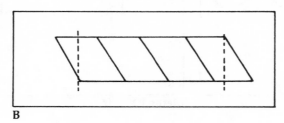

Picot Edging (Prairie Points)

This decorative edging is long wearing (four layers of material) and very easily made. It is known as "picot edging" in Canada and as "prairie points" in the United States. This useful edging can also double as decorative closures (see page 51).

Note: Most project items in this book will look best with a 4" (10 cm) square picot edge. Use a larger square, 6" (15 cm) or 8" (20 cm) for adult-size quilts, and use the 4" (10 cm) square for baby quilts.

1. Cut a number of 4" (10 cm) squares. Be sure they are truly *square* (A). To figure out the number you need to make, put together three, at the space interval you want (close together or farther apart), and measure how much space they cover. Measure the perimeter of the edges you wish to cover and divide your first figure into the second. For example, my edging sample covers a space of 3" (7.5 cm) and I have to cover 30" (75 cm) so I need to make ten squares. *Note:* Two methods of making edging are illustrated below.

2. Fold the squares in half and press and then fold in half again (B).

3. Sitting at the sewing machine, place the folded squares together. Sew halfway down each, one at a time.

4. Put together all of your squares in one long string (C).

5. Then with the raw edges of the picot edging to the raw edge of the top layer of the garment, push aside the under layers and sew on by machine (D).

6. Curve the corners of your project for easiest application .

7. Fold raw edge to inside and whipstitch the back to the picot edges, being sure not to stitch right through to the front .

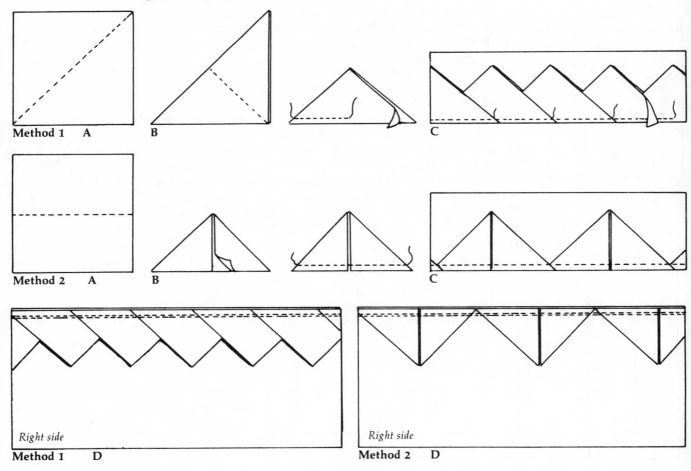

Lining a Vest

This method is the simplest way to line a vest.

Method 1
Hand Finishing

1. Use the pressed, embellished vest pieces of the outer shell (before they are made up) as the pattern for the lining. After making up the outer shell proceed with the next steps.
2. With the right sides of the vest lining together, machine sew the shoulder seams. Press the seams open and zigzag or otherwise finish the seams.
3. With the right sides together, machine sew the underarm seams. Press open and finish the seams so they will not fray.
4. Insert the lining into the vest shell, pinning and matching at the shoulder and underarm seams, *wrong sides together.*
5. Turn under the seam allowances on both the shell and the lining, turning under slightly more of the lining than the outer shell so that the lining does not show on the outside.
6. Using matching colored thread and a fine, close whipstitch, hand sew around the outer edges of the neckline, front edges, and around the lower hem. Stitches will mainly be on the inside.
7. In the same manner, turn the seam allowances of the armhole inside and whipstitch.
8. Press (A).

Machine Finishing

1.-4. Proceed as above until you are ready to turn under the seam allowances on the outer edge, neckline, and lower edge of the vest and the armholes.
5. Turn under as directed, remembering to turn the lining in slightly more so that it does not show, and pin at frequent intervals, having the straight pins at right angles to the material edge.
6. With the straight sew pressor foot on, sew by machine and with a fine stitch — 10 to 12 stitches to the inch (2.5 cm) — sew a scant 1/4" (0.6 cm) from the folded edge.
7. For a more sporty effect, sew a second line of machine sewing 1/8" (0.3 cm) inside the first (B).
8. Press well before wearing.

Note: For a more decorative finish, cut and assemble the vest and lining to the stage where they are pinned together (lining and outer shell). Then make up double-fold bias binding as shown on page 57 and apply, treating the outer shell and the lining as one fabric. The bias binding can be a contrast to or match with any of the materials in the vest.

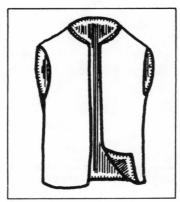

A

B

inside lining

Method 2

Using the outer shell of the vest as your pattern, cut the front and back pieces for the lining.

1. Sew the shoulder seams on the outer vest and the lining, page 63 (A).

2. Trim the lining all around by 1/8" (0.3 cm) so that when inserted it does not droop.

3. Pin the outer vest and lining *right* sides together.

4. Machine sew around the outside edges using a 5/8" (1.5 cm) seam allowance but *do not sew the four side seams* (two on outer vest and two on lining). You will need these openings for turning the vest.

5. Trim seam allowance to 1/4" (0.6 cm).

6. Turn the vest right side out by pulling the front sections through, under the shoulder seams and out one back opening (B).

7. Press the edges flat, being sure that the lining is to the outside.

8. On one side seam of the outer shell, pin the vest front and back together (C).

9. From the opposite side, reach through to the middle of the vest and lining and take hold of the pinned side seam. Pull it through the middle and out the opposite side.

10. Match and pin the seams of the lining and then the vest being sure that the right sides are together (D).

11. Machine sew in a continuous line of sewing, stitching both the vest side and the lining side.

12. Now pull the finished side back through.

13. Pin the outer shell front to the outer shell back on the remaining side seam (E).

14. Draw it wrong side out as far as you can through the lining.

15. Start to stitch on the lining and towards the outer shell, in a circle.

16. Continue stitching as far as possible, ending the stitching on the lining piece, being sure to leave a 6" (15 cm) opening in the lining seam.

17. Pull the vest right side out (F).

18. Overlap and pin closed the 6" (15 cm) opening (G).

19. Hand stitch the opening shut using a whipstitch (H).

The summer psychedelic vest project on page 84 was assembled using the method pictured here.

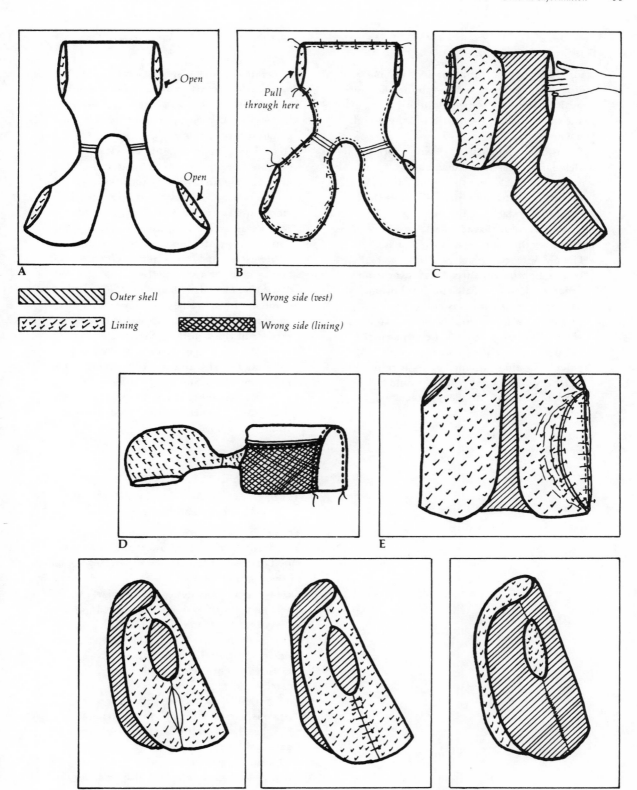

A

Open

Open

B

Pull
through here

C

Outer shell   Wrong side (vest)

Lining   Wrong side (lining)

D

E

F

G

H

TIPS   Use of Color

Your choice of color combinations can make your crazy patchwork more striking and more beautiful. Here are some helpful hints to make the color suit the fabric and the use of the patchwork.

- Traditional Victorian crazy patchwork used rich dark colors with much black.
- A patch of black next to a color will make it brighter; a patch of white will make the color look paler.
- Using one color thread on all the seams enhances the coloring of the patches.
- The old Victorian plan was to use up odd bits of embroidery threads left over from other work in true patchwork tradition. This meant a great many colors were used in one piece. If you do this, be sure to use a shade along each seam that contrasts with the patches on either side. Dark or bright patches would be divided by light colored stitchery while light patches would be bordered by dark stitchery thread.

- To create a modern "sporty" crazy patchwork look use many shades of denim blue plus ginghams and bright calicoes to harmonize. Use heavyweight thread with bright, primary colors.
- To achieve a modern dainty effect, use delicate floral prints, eyelet materials, bits of lace, and stitch with pastel silks.
- For a modern Christmas crazy patchwork "look" use red and green ginghams and calicoes as well as plain colors and Christmas prints. Combine these with white eyelet, and stitch in red, green, white, and/or gold for a smart effect.
- Black thread is also good.
- If you are using a fine embroidery thread such as #8 pearl cotton or two or three strands of floss, put together two shades, one light and one quite dark of the same color, and work a row of herringbone stitch.
- Try using a dark and a light color.
- The simple blanket stitch looks great when a dark and a light color of thread are used in the same needle

TIPS   How To Add Personality To Crazy Patchwork

Your crazy patchwork can be country or urban, subdued or flamboyant and express a mood or create a look by encorporating some of these hints:

- areas where patches are too angular, can be broken up with ovals, circles, shields, etc.,
- areas that are too "strippy," add such shapes as shields, octagons, hexagons, triangles, squares, rectangles, fan shapes,
- pictures can be created with crazy patchwork,
- memorabilia such as hair ribbons, prize ribbons, bits of lace, ribbon and trim, men's ties, lace handkerchiefs, scarves, etc., add a personal touch,
- jet beads, crystal beads, other beads and spangles, sequins, etc., can also be added, and
- fabric paints (Victorians used oil paints) will add interest to plain pieces of material.

WOMEN'S WEAR

San Diego Spring Jacket

This jacket was named "San Diego Spring" because I designed and started it in a creative clothing workshop with Virginia Avery in San Diego at the International Quilt Exhibition in 1981. The deep coral, dark and medium browns, terra cotta, and sage green combined with the deep aqua pick up the predominately desert colors of that delightful city.

Technique Used   Semi-Traditional with variation I

Techniques Suitable   Traditional, semi-traditional with variations I and II

Materials Required

2 yds (2 m) aqua cotton or cotton/polyester blend broadcloth 45″ (112.5 cm) wide

2-1/2 yds (2-1/2 m) deep coral cotton or cotton/polyester blend broadcloth 45″ (112.5 cm) wide

2 yds (2 m) polyester bonded quilt batting

1/4 yd (22.5 cm) dark background print with coral, beige, brown, pale green, aqua, and terra cotta (Choose your print first and bring your colors out of that print to harmonize and contrast.)

Scraps of cottons or cotton/polyester plains in the colors of the print

1 spool deep aqua #8 pearl cotton

1 spool each deep coral and aqua sewing thread

1 double-needle for your sewing machine

1/2 yd (45 cm) nonwoven fusible interfacing

1 spool brown or rust thread for machine embroidery

Fabric gluestick

Pattern Making

1. The pattern for a funnel-neckline, slightly flared, hip-length jacket is given here for you to enlarge (A). If you choose to use a commercial pattern with a similar style, be sure that it has a minimum of seams and darts.
2. Refer to pages 46, 47 for information on enlarging and making the pattern.
3. Enlarge the applique motifs in a similar manner.

Cutting

1. Cut out one back, two fronts, and one-third of the sleeve top in aqua.
2. Cut out one back, two fronts, and two full sleeves in coral.
3. Cut out one back, two fronts, and two full sleeves in quilt batting.

Laying Out

1. Lay the coral sleeve pieces *right side down* in front of you.
2. Over them lay the quilt batting pieces.
3. Lay the aqua top one-third of the sleeve pattern in place and secure with small gold safety pins.
4. Choose a color sequence for your scrap materials and arrange them in color piles.
5. Using the semi-traditional method with variation I (see page 17) and starting at the aqua sleeve portions, sew the crazy patchwork pieces on until the entire sleeve portion is covered.
6. Keep the scale of your pieces roughly equal and use the same number of repetitions of your pieces but not necessarily in the same place on each sleeve.

Embellishment

1. Stitches used on this jacket are plain blanket stitch; closed blanket stitch; plain and zigzag chain; herringbone; open cretan; fern stitch; single, double,

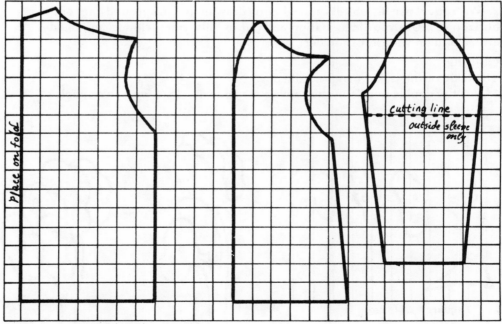

A   **1 square = 2" (5 cm)**

and triple featherstitch; star stitch; flat, straight stitch; and french knots. Look through the stitch combination charts for some especially fancy combinations to use on plain pieces of material.

2. As well, from your print scraps, cut out some motifs and applique them with a close buttonhole stitch to the larger plain pieces or to areas where some of your patches do not quite cover.

3. Sew around the shape of the sleeve with a close machine stitch before trimming the scraps to fit.

Applique by Machine
Jacket back and left front have applique design (B).

1. Cut a rectangle of material slightly larger than the applique pattern pieces and bond it to a lightweight fusible interfacing material. Use a damp cloth, a hot iron, and *press* (don't iron) for best results. Let the piece dry.

2. Pin applique pattern pieces to the material and cut out. No seam allowance is necessary if you are appliqueing by machine.

3. Arrange pieces in place on the back and left front of the jacket (C).

4. Hold in place with a fabric glue.

5. Applique, using a matching sewing thread and a satin stitch.

6. Before stitching in place, check the placement of the appliques, especially the front one to be sure the placement is flattering.

Making Up
1. Join the underarm seams of the outer jacket and then the same seams in the lining.

2. Press seams open.

3. With lining right side down, place the batting over it and the jacket piece right side up.

4. Pin baste carefully and frequently with small gold safety pins.

5. With an art pencil (white is good) lightly draw in the background lines of the horizon (C). Use your imagination and put in hills, trees, clouds, and maybe even a bird on your left shoulder.

Quilting
The body of the jacket may be quilted.

1. Put the double needle in the sewing machine and load with two spools of

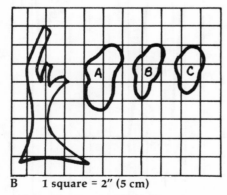

B   1 square = 2" (5 cm)

A Cut 2 print and 2 plain
B Cut 4 print
C Cut 2 plain
Tree cut two brown

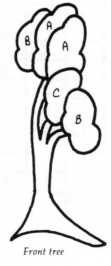

Front tree   Back tree

aqua thread. If your machine does not have two spindles for thread, put a plastic straw over the one spindle and place the spools of thread one above the other and thread your needle.

2. Set the stitch tension slightly looser than usual and the stitch length to 8 or 9 stitches to the inch (2.5 cm). Practise on a scrap "textile sandwich."

3. Quilt around the applique about 1/8" (0.3 cm) away from it, "echo-style." Be careful finishing off the threads to be sure the finish is neat. It is usually best to bring the top thread through to the back and tie off, clipping short.

4. Starting at one side of the jacket and working across to the other side, quilt the background — trees, horizon, etc. Try to start and finish at a raw edge as much as possible so there are a minimum of clipped ends. Always quilt in the same direction, otherwise unsightly ripples will result.

Finishing

1. With right sides together, sew the shoulder seams.

2. Using double-fold bias stripping made from the coral broadcloth (see instructions on page 57), trim seam and hand stitch the binding over the raw edge. (Always finish a garment piece as far as you can in each step.)

3. With right sides of the sleeves together, sew the sleeve seams. Finish the seam edges as above.

4. Baste sleeves into armhole being sure to ease out any slight fullness.

5. Check for correct fit, then cover the seams as above.

6. Try on the jacket again and check sleeve and bottom edge length. Correct.

7. Starting at the back neck centre, apply double-fold bias binding (coral) with raw edges of binding pinned to raw edge of right side of jacket.

8. Machine stitch.

9. Turn folded edge of binding under and hand stitch to jacket lining.

10. Finish sleeves in the same way.

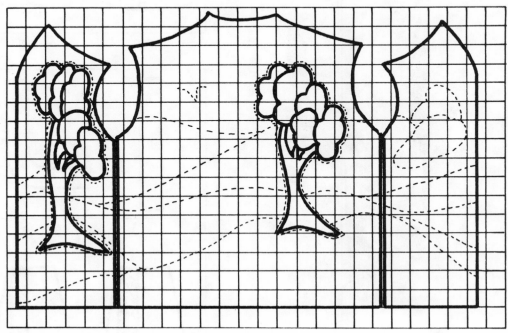

C   - - - - - - *Quilting design*

Wraparound Skirt and Bolero

I have several of these outfits made of a heavy cotton garbardine and trimmed with various types of patchwork. I enjoy all of them but the one photographed here is my favorite. Teamed with a soft blouse, a crisp shirt, or a turtleneck sweater I can make the outfit dressy or casual and it is always flattering. The wraparound skirt is easily adjusted to your girth and the bolero is an easy, one-piece construction. The bolero and skirt can have a rounded edge or square-cornered edge on the right front wrapover (see diagrams A, B, C). You'll want to make several in different colors.

Technique Used Semi-traditional

Techniques Suitable All

Materials Required

2-1/2 yds (2-1/2 m) cotton or wool gabardine, cotton poplin, denim, brushed colored denim, or any medium-weight material that is 45" (112.5 cm) wide

Scraps of material for crazy patchwork (Choose cottons and blends for daytime outfits and silks, satins, etc., for dressier outfits.)

1 ball red #8 pearl cotton

1 yd (1 m) of coordinating or contrasting cotton or blend for bias binding

1 spool sewing thread

Velcro for waist closure in the same color as the skirt (optional)

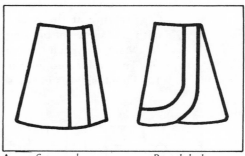

A   *Square edge*   *Rounded edge*

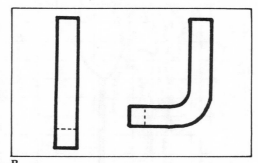

B

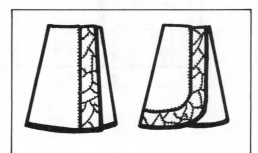

C

Pattern Making

1. Refer to the sketches given here and the pattern-making techniques discussed on pages 46, 47. Use nonwoven materials such as Trace-a-Pattern™ to enlarge the design.
2. Cut it out completely (i.e. not just half the pattern).
3. Machine baste together and try on. Adjust for fit.
4. Would the bolero look better if it were longer? Shorter? Add to the Trace-a-Pattern™ for length or width or fold up the amount you think you want to take out.
5. Try it on again and adjust.
6. Use this as the pattern for the skirt and bolero.

Making Up

Skirt

1. Machine sew darts.
2. Machine sew the two fronts to the back, press seams, and finish (see page 55).
3. Try on, pin closed. Wearing the shoes you plan to wear with it, adjust the length.

The bolero pattern is the same as that used for the "stained glass" vest, page 79.

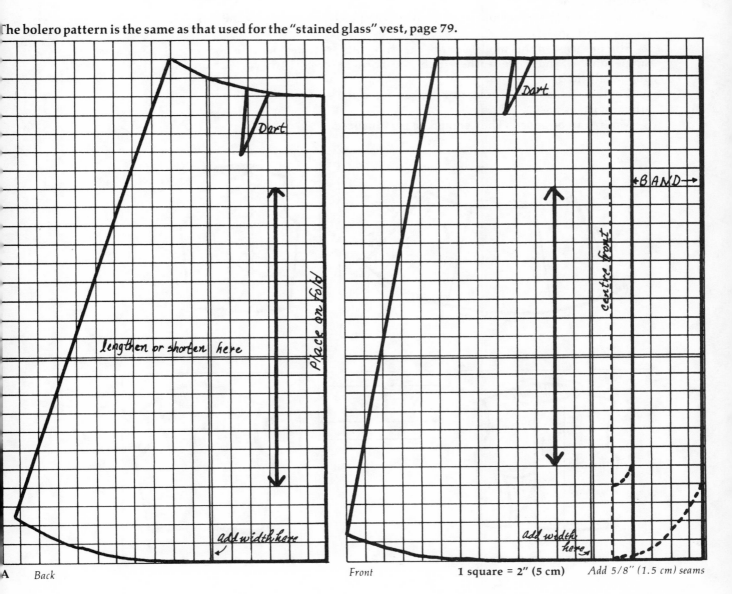

A   *Back*   *Front*   **1 square = 2" (5 cm)**   *Add 5/8" (1.5 cm) seams*

Bolero

1. Machine sew the shoulder seams on the bolero, press open, and finish.
2. Try on and correct the fit if necessary.

Skirt Trim

1. Make a paper pattern of the front edge of the right front so that it is about 2" (5 cm) longer than the skirt (to allow for the embroidery "taking up" the material) and 6" (15 cm) wide (B).
2. Cut one from foundation fabric.

Bolero Trim

1. Make a paper pattern of the right front edge so that it is about 2" (5 cm) longer than the edge to be trimmed and 6" (15 cm) wide.
2. Cut one from foundation material.

Laying Out

1. Lay out the scraps in a pleasing collage, using the principles discussed on page 16.
2. Pin and baste, underlapping and overlapping as necessary.

Embellishment

1. Using red #8 pearl cotton, work around each patch and embellish the plain patches with motifs.
2. Stitches used in this model are the chevron stitch; tête de boeuf; fishbone; single, double, and triple featherstitch; sheaf stitch; scroll stitch; cable chain; and petal stitch.
3. Combinations of stitches can be taken from the section on combination stitches, pages 36-42.
4. Motifs can be added. They should be personalized.

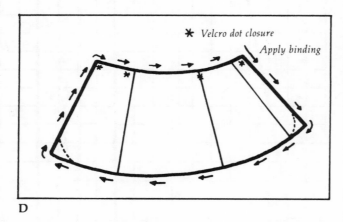

D

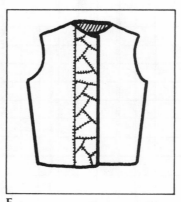

E

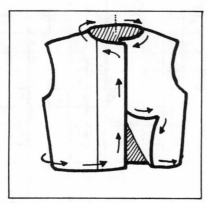

F

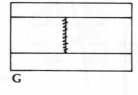

G

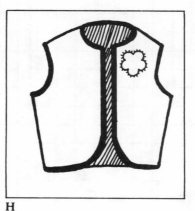

H

Finishing

1. Press both strips of patchwork, face down, on a turkish towel.
2. Pin in place (right side up) on the bolero and skirt. Trim to fit if necessary.
3. Turn under the raw edge opposite the raw edge of the skirt. Baste and press.
4. Using the same color embroidery thread, work one of your favorite stitches down the seamline to secure it. Do not pull too tightly or it will pucker (C).
5. Use the bias binding you have made (see directions page 57) and apply it to the edge, starting at the right front and working continously around to the upper left front (D). Hand or machine finish. Velcro dot closures were used in the photograph. Bind waistband.

Finishing the Bolero

1. Apply the trim in the same manner as for the skirt (E).
2. Apply the binding in the same manner, starting at the back neck edge (F), turning under the raw end, and continuing around to the same spot, again, turning under the raw end.
3. Hand or machine finish, sewing the join at the back neck by hand (G).

Note: On the rounded edge of the bolero, you may choose to cut an applique motif out of a piece of crazy patchwork and applique that on the left shoulder area instead of using a band trim (H).

Sarah Jane's Wedding Dress
Prom Dress, Bridesmaid Dress, Party Dress

Princess Diana popularized these enormous bouffant sleeves at her wedding. They are romantic, feminine, and very easily made. The dress of polyester silk-like material looks fragile and dainty but wears beautifully and hardly creases. Use a commercial pattern for the dress with the bouffant sleeves.

Technique Used Traditional

Technique Suitable Traditional

Materials Required (for the trim only)

Scraps of velvet, silk, ribbons, and lace in the color scheme of your choice. The photograph shows burgundy, turquoise, purple, mauve, blue, ecru, and the pink from the dress. Keep the scraps under 2" (5 cm) in diameter for a dainty effect.

1 ball each medium pink (to match the dress) and turquoise #8 pearl cotton

Lace medallions (the ones I used are from my wedding dress)

If you have any antique lace in your family, this is the place to use it.

5 yds (5 m) of 2" (5 cm) wide burgundy satin ribbon and 5 yds (5 m) of 1" (2.5 cm) burgundy satin ribbon and 2 yds (2 m) tatted lace

Pattern Making

1. Cut two lengths of sheeting the width of the sleeve (before making up) and 2-1/2" (6.25 cm) wide (A).

Laying Out

1. Arrange the scraps in a repetitive order of color, even though all the materials may not be identical. The order used here is burgundy, turquoise, purple, pink, mauve, blue, and ecru. Then repeat this order.

Pinning and Basting

1. Pin and baste to the strip of sheeting.

Embellishment

1. Using the pink thread — I used a variety of stitches such as herringbone; cross-stitch; double, single, and triple featherstitch; chain; zigzag chain; alternating chain (with turquoise); flat stitch; fern stitch; detached and attached fly stitch. Keep the scale of the stitches small to suit the trim.

2. Edges of the strip remain raw, but trim to size.

3. Over a plain scrap tack a lace medallion (use three or five and space them evenly).

4. Using the turquoise and pink threads, work decorative stitches to hold the medallions in place.

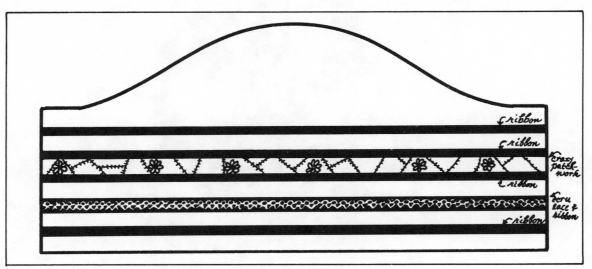

A

Making Up

1. Across the widest part of the sleeve pin the worked strip of crazy patchwork (A).
2. Pin a 1" (2.5 cm) wide burgundy ribbon in place to cover the raw edge, top and bottom. Use matching burgundy sewing thread and tack in place.
3. 2" (5 cm) away, top and bottom, lay the widest burgundy satin ribbon and tack in place.
4. Lay the ecru lace (Grandmother's tatted lace edging was used for the dress in the photograph) and tack it in place with matching thread in the centre of the ribbon.
5. 1" (2.5 cm) above and below this strip, tack in place the narrow burgundy ribbon.

Finishing

1. Make up the sleeve as usual, making sure that the ribbons match at the seamline.

Note: The burgundy bridesmaid's dress is worked in the same way but there is no tatted lace nor lace medallions and the ribbons used are medium pink. You could use a variety of white silks, moiré, taffeta, crepes, pongee, novelty weaves, brocade, lace, etc., and embellish with white silk or shiny white rayon thread for a subtle, white-on-white effect for the traditional bride.

Sash

1. Cut a piece of the dress material 3 yds (3 m) long and 7" (17.5 cm) wide. You may have to piece it but that is fine.
2. Fold in half (B).
3. Move the left corner down until it forms a triangle (C). Try this out with a scrap of material before you attempt the sash.
4. Start to sew at point X and gently pull the material down to seam it as you go along. You will end up with a tube sewn on the bias with the seam spiraled around the tube (D).
5. Turn, press, and hand hem the ends.

Headdress

1. Cut a piece of the dress material 1 yd (1 m) long and cut it 4" (10 cm) wide. You will have to press it.
2. Fold and sew it as above.
3. Tie it in place around the forehead or around the crown of the head as shown in the photograph, ending in a bow with ends hanging down about 3" (7.5 cm).

Note: The dress (in white with white-on-white crazy patchwork embroidery), sash, and headdress would be perfect for a confirmation outfit.

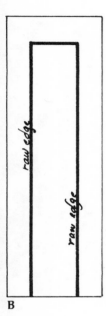

B

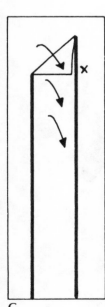

C

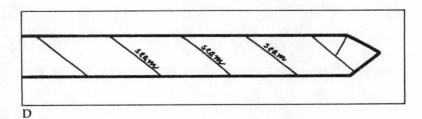

D

Crazy Patchwork Trimmed Skirt and Blouse

Made to display one's love of patchwork and fancy stitching, this matching blouse and skirt could not be easier to make nor more flattering to the wearer.

Technique Used Traditional

Technique Suitable Traditional

Materials Required

3-1/2 yds (3-1/4 m) of 42" (105 cm) wide rose polyester/cotton blend broadcloth with small navy and white windowpane checks

Scraps of plain navy and rose broadcloth and a variety of rose and navy prints and stripes (In the model all the scraps are from a coordinated collection.)

1 ball medium blue #8 pearl cotton

1/2 yd (45 cm) of nonfusible interfacing, light- or medium-weight

Hook and eye for skirt closing

Rose sewing thread

Pattern Making

1. Find a commercial pattern with a boat neckline, sleeves cut in one with the bodice, and a dirndl-style skirt in your own size.

2. Using the neckline on the front and back bodice pieces, trace off the outline onto tissue paper or Trace-a-Pattern™. Add at least 4" (10 cm) all around to form a decorative outer facing. In the photographs here the front and back facings are slightly different in shape for easy identification when dressing.

3. Experiment with several facing styles (A).

Cutting

1. Cut out the blouse and skirt pieces.

2. Cut out the front and back facings from interfacing.

3. Measure the circumference of the sleeves and cut two strips this length and 3" (7.5 cm) wide.

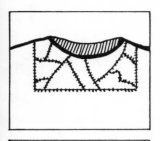

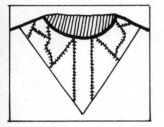

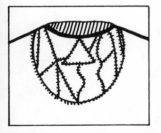

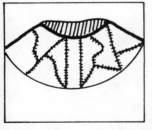

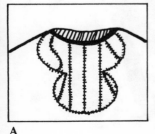

A

Pinning and Basting

1. Baste blouse together, try on for fit, and sew by machine.
2. Baste skirt together, try on for fit, and sew by machine.
3. Baste shoulder seams of the outer facings; check for fit and proper placement of shape of facing.
4. Machine sew shoulder seams on the facing and press seams open.

Embellishment

1. Pin scraps in place on the outer neckline and sleeve facings.
2. Be sure to distribute the solid colors, especially the navy, evenly and attractively.
3. Follow the directions for traditional technique on page 16.
4. Stitches used are star stitch; french knots; single, double, and triple featherstitch; open cretan with fly stitch; "lazy daisy" stitch; fern stitch; closed buttonhole; straight stitch with french knots in flower shape; herringbone stitch; zigzag chain; and outline stitch.

Making Up
Blouse

1. Turn under 1/4" (0.6 cm) all around the outside edge of the outer facing and baste and press.
2. Pin the facing in place *over* the blouse and finish the neckline with a narrow, double-fold bias binding in the same rose, navy, and white material. (See page 57 for making bias binding.)
3. Seam together, wrong sides together, the short edges of the sleeve facings. Check to be sure they are an exact fit.
4. Pin the facings in place so that they flip over and the right side is out and the seam is hidden.
5. Machine sew in place.

Finishing

1. With a double featherstitch attach the pressed-under edges of the outer facing to the blouse.
2. With a double featherstitch attach the pressed-under edges of the sleeve facings to the cap sleeves.
3. Hem the bottom of the blouse.

Making Up
Skirt

1. Gently gather the top edge of the front and back of the skirt.
2. Sew the side seams, attaching the pocket flaps as shown in the diagram.
3. Measure your waist and add 4" (10 cm).
4. Cut the waistband this length and 4" (10 cm) wide.
5. Turn the band in half with right sides together (add interfacing if you like) using the same measurements but only 2" (5 cm) wide.
6. Sew across the short ends, clip, and turn.
7. Press. Then press a 1/2" (1.25 cm) seam allowance under each long edge.
8. Pin waistband to the skirt, leaving opening on left side, and adjusting gathers.
9. Turn back 2" (5 cm) on the front side and bring the back piece right out over the pocket flap.
10. Sew on a hook and eye for closure.
11. Allow the skirt to hang on a hanger for twenty-four hours, then even up the hem and machine hem with a narrow hem.

Crazy Patchwork "Stained Glass" Vest

Because this technique is fast and the product so attractive, consider making matching his and hers vests for formal occasions.

Technique Used   Machine method

Techniques Suitable   All

Materials Required

1 yd (1 m) lightweight cotton

1 yd (1 m) turquoise polyester/silk lining

Scraps of materials in burgundy, turquoise, grey, plum, rose, dark grey, navy, and black. This is an opportunity to use some prints that are larger in scale because the scraps should be from 3" (7.5 cm) by 4" (10 cm) to 6" (15 cm) in size. For a small woman, keep the size of the scraps at the lower end of the size range; for a tall man, the pieces may be larger.

Materials used in the photograph here include grey Ultrasuede™, plush, velveteen, corduroy, tie silk, and several different textures of polyester double knit.

2 large spools burgundy thread (polyester-wrapped cotton core sewing thread is best)

1 small spool turquoise polyester-wrapped cotton core sewing thread

Fabric gluestick

Pattern Making

1. Refer to the section on pattern making. Draw the pattern (A), cut it out of muslin or Trace-a-Pattern™ adding 1" (2.5 cm) per pattern piece to allow for the "taking up" of the material when sewing.

2. Machine-baste, fit, and use as the cutting pattern.

3. Alternatively, choose a waist-length vest pattern *one size larger* than your regular size (again to allow "taking up").

Cutting

1. Cut out two fronts and one back from the foundation material. Be *sure* to add the seam allowance. Seam side seams.

2. Cut out two fronts and the back in silk.

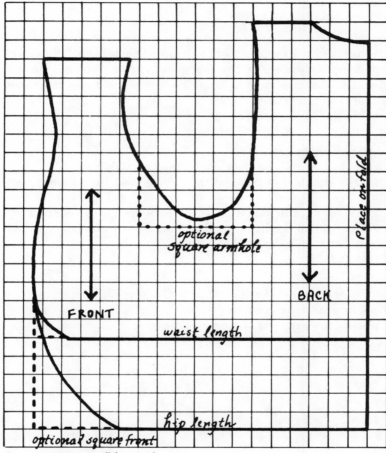

A   1 square = 1" (2.5 cm)

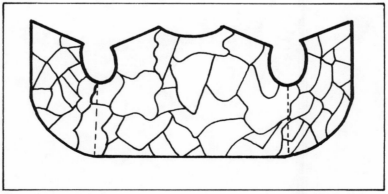

B

Laying Out

1. Separate your scraps by color and determine a color sequence. Starting at the left upper corner of each front and the back, lay out the scraps in a pleasing design, correcting the color sequence as necessary for good visual effect (B).
2. There is no need to hem under the scraps as they will be covered by the stitching. Working is easier, however, if you *underlap* the heavier pieces.
3. When satisfied with the design, glue baste the pieces into position.
4. With a wide zigzag stitch baste them in place because you will be handling the piece a great deal and glue basting will not suffice.

Embellishment

1. Using burgundy thread on top and any left-over colored thread in the bobbin (be sure the tension is right so that the bobbin thread is not "pulled up" to show on top) completely cover all the raw edges with a close and smooth machine satin stitch. You may have to go over some seams twice to get the smooth effect that is so important.
2. Pull threads through to the back, tie, and clip.

Making Up

1. Seam shoulders of shell.
2. Press the outer shell of the vest, face down, on a turkish towel.
3. Sew together the shoulder seams and the side seams of the lining, press well.
4. With the right sides together starting at the back neck, sew together the lining and outer shell, down the fronts, and around the bottom. Leave a small opening 6" (15 cm) for turning at the back neck.
5. Turn and press well.

Finishing

1. With a small, neat overcast stitch and turquoise thread, turn in the raw edges of the back neck and the armholes.
2. Press well, placing the garment face down on a towel.

"Stained glass" vest project, page 78.

Victoriana party vest project, page 82.

San Diego Spring jacket project, page 66, and matching tote bag project, page 133.

Square Armhole vest project, page 86. Matching handbag project, page 135.

Victoriana Party Vest

Rich glowing colors and luxurious fabrics combine to make this thigh-length, U-necked open vest the backbone of your winter party wardrobe. Rich shades of red, gold, brown, black, blue, orange, rust, grey, and navy in many different colors and textures are highlighted by gold-colored embroidery. Team the vest with a black jersey skirt and black silk turtleneck sweater for a sophisticated outfit or wear it with a rich, nut-brown wool sweater and slacks for a casual, but elegant country look. This vest can also add flair to grey flannel pants or long skirt and a grey silk blouse, or wear the vest with a ruby red silk jersey dress with long sleeves for a festive, party look.

Technique Used   Traditional

Techniques Suitable   All

Materials Required

1-1/2 yds (1-1/2 m) of 45" (112.5 cm) wide foundation fabric
1/4 yd (22.5 cm) each of black velvet, brown plush, grey flannel, red velvet
Scraps of tie silk, novelty brocades, Ultrasuede™, novelty polyester knits (Avoid fragile fabrics such as lamé and sheers.)
1-1/2 yds (1-1/2 m) of black silk lining
1 ball gold-colored #5 or #8 pearl cotton
1 spool black polyester-wrapped cotton core sewing thread

Pattern Making

You may choose to buy a commercial pattern or make a pattern from the diagram given here (A). If you choose a commercial pattern, look for a thigh-length plain vest with a slight flare at the hips. Be sure to purchase the pattern one size larger than your regular size to allow for the "taking up" of the stitching. If you choose to make a pattern from the sketch provided, refer to page 46.

Cutting
1. Cut out two fronts and a back from the foundation material.
2. Cut out two fronts and a back from the lining material.

Laying Out
1. Divide your scraps into piles of similar colors. You can use different materials but remember to keep the color values the same.
2. Lay out all three pieces (two fronts and the back) at the same time.
3. Be sure that the same color appears on each of the three pieces, but not in exactly the same place.
4. Arrange your collage of scraps into a visually pleasing and balanced order.

Pinning and Basting
1. When you are satisfied with your arrangement pin it in place and then hand or machine baste down, underlapping and overlapping materials as necessary. It is necessary to baste down the pieces while you work on them or they fall off causing untold annoyance.
2. If you wish, you can arrange to have a plain piece of velvet in the underarm area where brushing of the arm causes a great deal of wear.

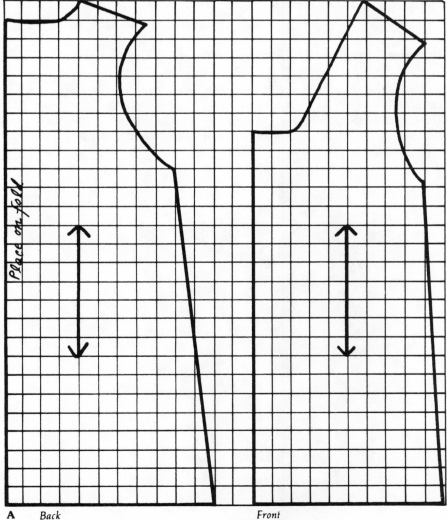

A   *Back*   *Front*
1 square = 1" (2.5 cm)   *Add 5/8" (1.5 cm) seams*

Embellishment

1. Stitches used for the photographed vest include single, double, and triple featherstitch; open cretan stitch; star stitch; detached fly stitch; sheaf stitch; cross-stitch; herringbone stitch; detached chain stitch; fern stitch; couching; running stitch; wheatear stitch; tête de boeuf stitch. I used very few combination stitches, only the fly stitch with detached chain stitch.
2. In the original vest, I used gold-colored six-stranded embroidery cotton; however, I recommend gold-colored pearl cotton for best results.

Making Up

1. Machine sew the side and shoulder seams of the outer shell and press.
2. Machine sew the side and shoulder seams of the lining and press.
3. With right sides together, machine sew around the outer edge of the vest, leaving an 8" (20 cm) opening for turning.
4. Trim seams, turn, and press well.
5. Hand sew the edges together in the opening and around the armhole using a tiny whipstitch.

Finishing

1. Sew a large hook and eye neatly at the upper neck closing on the inside.
2. Attach gold-colored or black "frog" to outer side or pin on a large, plain gold pin.

Summer Psychedelic Crazy Patchwork Trimmed Vest

Even if you don't have a passion for purple, the strongly contrasting colors used in this summer vest pick up even the most tired summer wardrobe. Select two strongly contrasting colors that predominate in your wardrobe (red and blue or rose and navy perhaps) to make the vest a versatile item. The straight style and the hip length are flattering to every figure and team well with slacks, skirts, and dresses.

Technique Used   Traditional

Techniques Suitable   All except semi-traditional with variation I

Materials Required

1 yd (1 m) each of purple and orange cotton or cotton/polyester blend broadcloth

1 spool each purple and orange sewing thread

1 ball each purple and orange #8 pearl cotton (both slightly darker than the color of your material)

Assortment of fabric scraps of cotton, polyester silks, crepes, and fine knits in prints and plains in yellow, pink, turquoise, purple, and orange, each about 3" (7.5 cm) in size.

Pattern Making

1. Refer to the techniques of pattern making on page 46.
2. Enlarge the pattern given (A), using these techniques.
3. Try on for correct fit and adjust.

Cutting

1. Use the adjusted pattern for cutting out the pieces for the outer shell (purple). You should have two fronts, two front strips, and the back.

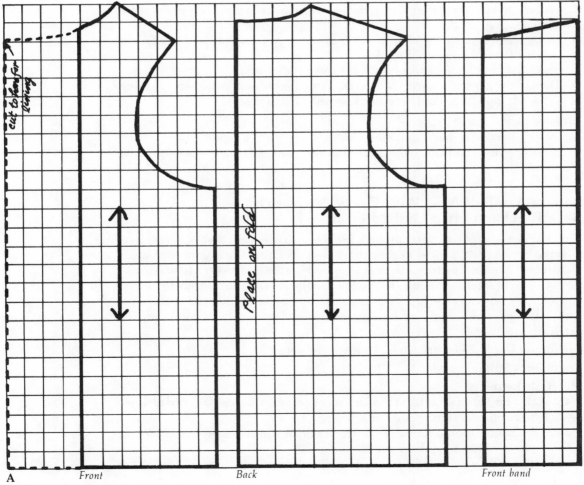

A

Front   *Back*   *Front band*

1 square = 1" (2.5 cm)   *Add 5/8" (1.5 cm) seam allowance*

Laying Out
1. Sort scraps by their dominant color.
2. Choose a color sequence and lay out the crazy pieces on the strips.
3. Lay out both strips at the same time, being careful to use the same color at least three times on each strip but not in exactly the same place. (This does not mean using the same prints or materials three times, only the *color*.)

Pinning and Basting
1. Overlap and underlap the pieces as necessary and pin them with small gold safety pins.
2. Turn under the raw edges and hand baste.

Embellishment
1. The stitches used on the seams of the photographed vest are single, double, and triple featherstitch; herringbone stitch; detached chain (daisy petals); wheatear stitch; attached and detached fly stitch; open cretan stitch; fern stitch; single chain with detached chains (see C I in "chain stitch combinations"), blanket stitch variations and combinations; star stitch; spanish knots; french knots; interlaced band stitch; and flat stitches in all combinations.

Making Up
1. Press the bands, face down, on a turkish towel.
2. With right sides together attach the bands to the fronts and press the seam to the back.
3. Using the pressed outer shell pieces (purple) as your pattern, cut two fronts and a back from the orange lining.
4. Seam the shoulder seams of both the purple shell and the orange lining.
5. Turn to the general information section and use the instructions for "Lining a Vest —Method 2" to complete the assembly of the vest.

Finishing
1. Do any necessary hand stitching.
2. Press the vest carefully, being sure that the orange lining *does not show to the front*.

Square Armhole Vest With Crazy Patchwork Back Panel and Strip Quilted Front

This warm and colorful vest can be a great wardrobe stretcher. Choose five different prints and plains, keying them to colors you already have in your wardrobe. The vest pictured is in cotton and cotton/polyester blend broadcloth (it's completely washable) in a turquoise floral print, purple pin dot, navy pin dot, grey tiny floral print, burgundy plain, and a plum print. The vest can be worn with pants or skirt and blouse or sweater in any of the colors in the patchwork.

Technique Used Semi-traditional with variation I
Techniques Suitable All
Materials Required
1/4 yd (22.5 cm) each of at least five different prints and one plain broadcloth
1 yd (1 m) turquoise floral print for lining
1/2 yd (45 cm) additional fabric of whichever print you choose for the binding
(Vest pictured has navy blue pin dot binding.)
1 yd (1 m) good quality *bonded* polyester quilt batting
1 large spool turquoise thread
1 ball purple #8 pearl cotton

Pattern Making

1. Refer to section on pattern making on page 46.

2. Draft the pattern pieces from the diagram (A), pin or baste, and try on for fit. Remember to add 1" (2.5 cm) to each pattern piece for "taking up" of fabric. If you buy a commercial pattern, be sure to buy one size larger than usual for the same reason.

Cutting

1. Cut out the two fronts, two underarm pieces, and back from the turquoise print.

2. Cut the same from the quilt batting. If you prefer a less bulky vest, split the batting in half horizontally.

Laying Out

1. Lay the lining, right side down, on the table and top with batting.

2. If your machine foot catches on the batting, put a piece of cellophane tape around the toe.

3. I started in the centre of the back panel because I wanted to use two blocks (small) left over from a coordinated pieced jacket.

4. You can add a strip of plain around the panel to set it off if you like.

5. Working outwards from these and using the semi-traditional technique with variation I of piecing, arrange your scraps in a pleasing design (B). Remember that with this type of piecing you get a very angular design; so perhaps you would like to applique a curved piece over the join of two pieces when finishing off the hand work.

6. Remember to start and end your machine stitching neatly. Pull threads to the back and tie off; they will hardly show in the floral print of the lining.

7. Lay aside the back panel and make up the fronts and side pieces by machine.

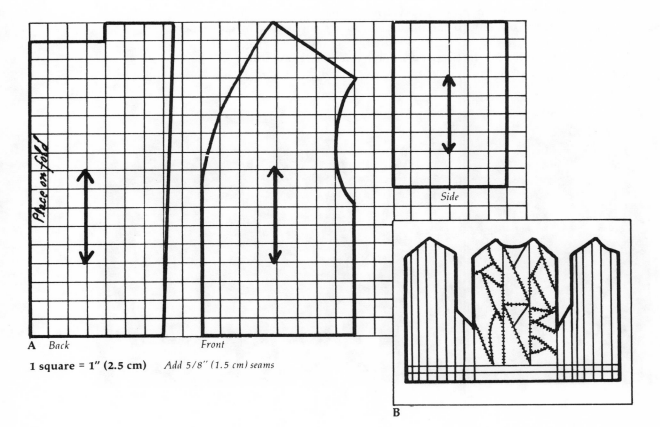

A *Back*   *Front*   *Side*

1 square = 1" (2.5 cm)   *Add 5/8" (1.5 cm) seams*

Place on fold

B

8. Cut strips of all your prints and plains the width of your fabric and 2″ (5 cm) wide. Lay lining right side down and top with batting.

9. Lay one strip (I used the navy pin dot as my central strip to coordinate with the binding) along the centre of each front and pin in place.

10. Using the pressed-piecing machine method (see page 16) and working outward from the centre strip, add your other pieces. Be sure each front is identical. Do the same with the two underarm pieces.

11. Trim to the pattern shape.

Embellishment

1. This technique often looks best if you embellish only about one-third of the joins. Try it, but if you want more, continue to embellish.

2. The stitches used on this vest are fern stitch, star stitch, open cretan stitch, single and double blanket stitch, featherstitch, and herringbone stitch. Use your imagination and create new combinations of the basic stitches.

Making Up

1. With right sides together, machine sew a 5/8″ (1.5 cm) seam on the shoulders and the two underarm seams.

2. Refer to page 55 for methods of finishing the seams. The photographed vest has seams finished by trimming off one side of the seam allowance and batting, and then turning under the raw edge of the remaining seam allowance over the raw seam either by machine or by hand.

Finishing

1. Make a bias binding, double for long wear (refer to page 57).

2. With raw edges of the binding pinned to the raw edge of the vest, *on the right side,* and starting from the centre back neck, machine stitch with 1/4″ (0.6 cm) seam allowance.

3. Turn under last raw edge at centre back neck.

4. Trim seams closely if necessary and either by hand or by machine sew the folded edge of the binding to the inside. If you are sewing by machine, sew from the top and use the "stitch-in-the-ditch" technique (see page 59).

5. Repeat for armholes, starting and stopping at centre underarm.

Note: I like to sew a 5″ (12.5 cm) by 4″ (10 cm) pocket on the inside left side for a hankie, keys, etc.

Crazy Patchwork Hat and Matching Ski Vest Trim

This gay and colorful ski hat is warm and allows your head to "breathe" thereby saving your hair from becoming damp and limp. It can be adapted for women, children, men, and boys. It is shown here in the women's version.

Technique Used   Semi-traditional with variation I

Techniques Suitable   All (with some adaptations)

HAT

Materials Required

1/4 yd (22.5 cm) of 45" (112.5 cm) wide cotton or blend broadcloth in ski suit color (for lining of hat)
1/4 yd (22.5 cm) of bonded quilt batting
1/4 yd (22.5 cm) of 45" (112.5 cm) foundation material
1/2 ball yarn in color of your choice for pom-pom
Scraps of material no larger than 3" (7.5 cm) in diameter
1 ball royal blue #8 pearl cotton

Pattern Making

1. This is so easy you don't even need a pattern! Just measure your head size and add 3" (7.5 cm) for seams and ease.
2. Measure from the crown of your head to the tip of your earlobe for the total depth of the hat and add 3" (7.5 cm) for the gathering at the top.

Cutting

1. Using these dimensions, cut a long rectangle of the lining material, the foundation material, and the quilt batting.

Laying Out

1. Arrange your scraps in piles by color, regardless of the pattern.
2. Select a sequence.
3. Lay out the scraps on the foundation material, arranging your collage until you are pleased (A). Use *half* the quilt batting (split horizontally).

Making Up

1. Using the technique described on page 17, sew down patches.
2. Baste down those seams that you cannot sew down with the machine.

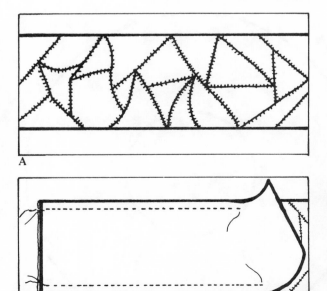

Embellishment

1. On the seams that need to be tacked down, use the herringbone stitch, single and double featherstitch, closed and open buttonhole, blanket stitch, and add any stitch combinations taken from the stitch combination section that are suitable. Children's hats should of necessity be more simple (they lose them and you may not want to put so much work on them). Women's and men's hats, in contrast, can be as elaborate as you like. On the woman's hat shown in the photograph some of the stitch combinations include chain stitches I, II, VI, and open cretan stitches IV and VI. (See pages 36, 40.)

Making Up the Hat

1. Lay the pieced outside of the hat *right side up* on the table. On it lay the lining piece, right side down.
2. On top of these lay a single layer (or the half layer) of quilt batting.
3. Machine sew the two long sides together, trim seams, and turn (B).
4. With right sides *out,* sew the short ends together in a narrow seam (C).
5. Turn inside out and machine sew this seam again so that all the raw edges are enclosed (D).
6. With a buttonhole or quilting thread doubled, gather the top of the hat evenly and fasten off securely (E).

Finishing the Hat

1. Try on hat placing the seam at the back.
2. Fit the back seam to the curve of the head by pinning (F).

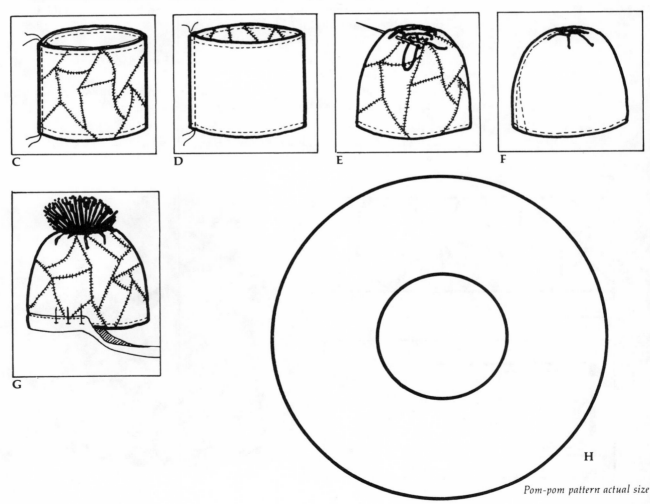

Pom-pom pattern actual size

3. Remove hat and machine sew a tapered seam so that the hat fits snugly but not too tightly around the head and over the ears. Machine sew a bias binding around the base of the hat to cover the bottom edge (G).

4. Make a large pom-pom and add to the gathered edge of the hat (G). Pom-pom directions are included below.

Note: Don't like pom-poms? Make a large bow of the lining material and top the hat with this, being sure to cover the gathering stitches.

Making a Pom-Pom

1. Cut two cardboard circles about 3" (7.5 cm) in diameter (H).
2. In the centre of each, cut out a small circle.
3. Using the yarn, wind around the circle evenly in two or three layers. The more yarn you use, the fluffier your pom-pom (I).
4. Cut between the two circles carefully but *do not remove* cardboard yet.
5. Tie a short length of the yarn to secure the pom-pom at the edge of the small circle.
6. Remove cardboard and shake pom-pom to fluff it up.
7. Trim with scissors if necessary for a nicely rounded shape.

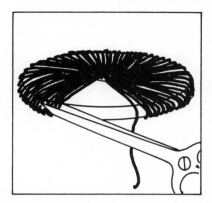

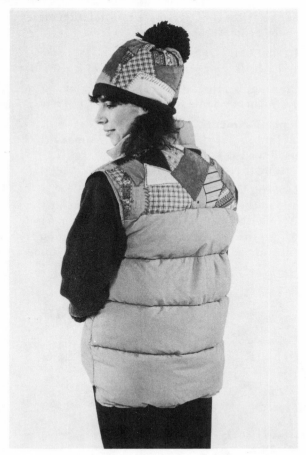

I

SKI VEST TRIM

Purchase a down or polyfibre-filled ski vest (watch for sales) in a color that coordinates or contrasts with your ski suit.

Materials Required

Scraps of materials to match those used in the vest (Remember to match the hat if you wish to coordinate them.)
1/4 yd (22.5 cm) soft foundation material
1 ball royal blue #8 pearl cotton
1 yd (1 m) wax paper, cut in half along the short measurement

Pattern Making

1. If the vest has a yoke, lay a piece of the wax paper over the yoke and pin in place.
2. With your fingers, sharply crease the outline of the yoke.
3. With a ruler, add 1/2" (1.25 cm) seam allowance and cut out the pattern.
4. Repeat for back yoke if there is one.
5. If there is no yoke, estimate the distance that you would want the trim to extend, measure carefully and make a paper pattern or measure out the length and width of the strip of your foundation material, being sure to add enough to shape around the neckline.

Laying Out

1. Lay out your scraps as described for the hat (A).

Pinning, Basting, Sewing

1. Using the same technique as for the hat, make the pattern piece.

Embellishment

1. Embroider all or some of the seams with the same color of pearl cotton as used for the hat.
2. Use the same stitches.

Making Up

1. Pin the pieces in place and baste under the seam allowance.
2. Sew the shoulder seam, usually by machine.
3. Pin the yoke in place and with matching thread and a fine applique stitch, turn under the raw edges all around, shaping around the neckline.

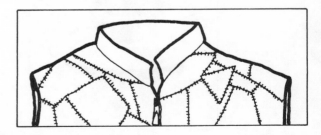

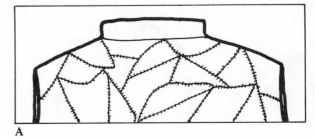

A

This family ensemble features the men's denim work shirt project, page 95, toddler's sweetheart jacket and hat project, page 108, and the ladies' wraparound skirt and bolero project, page 70.

Ski vest and hat project, page 89.

Sarah Jane's wedding dress project, page 73.

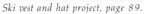

Crazy Patchwork Trimmed Caftan
Hostess Gown

Choose a simple pattern with a round neck and adapt it to this super-simple gown. The loose lines are cool and flattering to everyone.

Technique Used   Semi-Traditional

Techniques Suitable   Traditional, semi-traditional, machine method, and modern materials machine method.

Materials Required
Commercial caftan pattern with round or bateaux neckline
Yardage as required by pattern.
1/2 yd (45 cm) of medium-weight nonfusible interfacing (nonwoven)
1 ball royal blue #8 pearl cotton
Scraps of striped and floral cottons in pink, rose, navy, and light blue
Tissue paper or Trace-a-Pattern™ for making outer facing pattern
Rose sewing thread, cotton-wrapped with polyester

Pattern Making
1. Trace the neckline of the front and back bodice facing pieces.
2. Add 3" (7.5 cm) all around and extend down the front (A).
3. Tape together and try on (it should slip over your head).
4. Measure the circumference of the sleeves and cut two strips this length by 3" (7.5 cm) wide.

Cutting
1. Cut out the front, back, and sleeves of the caftan.
2. Cut the front and back facings (that you have designed from nonwoven interfacing).

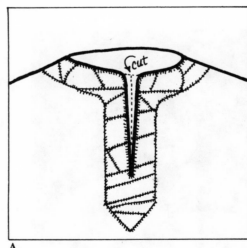

A

Laying Out

1. Arrange the scraps of material so that they form a pleasing design. Be sure to balance your very light and very dark scraps.
2. Using the pressed piecing procedure and starting at the centre back, piece by machine. (See semi-traditional method on page 16.)
3. Trim the edges to conform with the interfacing shape and press well.
4. In the same manner proceed with the sleeve facings.

Embellishment

1. Royal blue #8 pearl cotton is used for the stitching. The stitches used are single, double, and triple featherstitch; herringbone stitch; open cretan; detached and attached fly stitch; zigzag chain; graduated, grouped blanket stitches; star stitch; fern stitch; and wheatear stitch.
2. Use any of your own favorite stitches to make this gown a unique creation.
3. Press under 1/4″ (0.6 cm) around outside edges.

Making Up

1. Sew the side seams of the caftan and the shoulder seams.
2. Set in the sleeves.
3. With right sides together and the facing *underneath,* baste, check for fit, and then machine sew the neckline opening, including the slash for neck opening (A).
4. Clip curved seams and flip facing to the right side.
5. Sew short ends of each sleeve facing.
6. With right side of facing to wrong side of sleeve, baste, check, and then machine sew to sleeves.
7. Press under 1/4″ (0.6 cm) of raw edge and baste to sleeve.

Finishing

1. With royal blue #8 pearl cotton, featherstitch folded edge to sleeves.
2. Featherstitch folded edges of facing to gown.
3. Press carefully.
4. Adjust length of gown and make a small machine hem.

MEN'S WEAR
Man's Crazy Patchwork Trim Denim Work Shirt

For any leisure-time activity, this colorful casual shirt will be a favorite with your favorite man. The shirt shown is in medium blues, navy, and a touch of red. Other suggested combinations are all maroons, primary colors, or mono-chromatic color schemes, including browns and beiges and other masculine colors. Colors and materials should reflect your man's tastes and life-style —sporty check and polka dots, paisley designs, stripes, and plains could all be suitable.

Technique Used   Traditional

Techniques Suggested   Traditional, semi-traditional I or II (if using padding split the batt horizontally to reduce the bulk), and machine methods

Materials Required

1 denim work shirt, preferably with a back and front yoke, that you have *washed*
Scraps of cotton or cotton/polyester blend fabrics in medium, royal, and navy blue checks (different sizes). Use plains, prints, and polka dots. You will also need a few scraps (about one-third of the total) of bright red — red plaid, red background with polka dots.
1 spool medium blue sewing thread
1 ball red #8 pearl cotton embroidery thread

Toddler's sweetheart jacket and hat project, page 108.

Projects: Lambie pie quilt and pillow, page 111; 3-piece feeding set, page 114; christening dress and bonnet, page 104; toddler's jacket and hat, page 108.

San Diego Spring jacket project, page 66.

Denim work shirt project, page 95.

Christening dress and bonnet project, page 104.

Left: Victoriana Christmas wreath project, page 119.
Right: Sewing ensemble project, page 158.

Pattern Making

No pattern is necessary as the scraps are applied directly to the yoke of the shirt, using it as the foundation fabric to eliminate bulk.

Laying Out

1. Divide your scraps in piles of blue, navy, and those with red in them. This will help you to select a color sequence.
2. Start laying out the scraps at the centre back neck of the yoke (under the collar) being sure to use the brightest and darkest pieces at least three times on the back and three on each front to achieve balance in your design.
3. When your collage is pleasing to you, pin it in place or use a fabric gluestick, underlapping and overlapping as necessary.
4. Hand baste in place, turning under raw edges where necessary.
5. Repeat for the front yokes, turning under the raw edges at the neckline, sleeveline, and along the yoke.

Embellishment

1. Embroider the seamlines, being sure to catch both sides of the seam.
2. Take as little thread as possible through to the back and *do not use knots* (anchor threads with two or three little stitches or pull small knots through so they rest between the outer yoke and the lining).
3. Elaborate stitch combinations are *not* suitable here. Use plain stitches such as attached chain, blanket stitch, zigzag stitch, and attached fly stitches varying them by size and closeness to one another.
4. Keep the tension adjusted so that the embroidery lies firmly on the top of the cloth where it will not catch on things.
5. Embellish some of the plain larger pieces with some appropriate symbols such as fish, ducks, dogs, nautical symbols, horses, cars, boats, etc. Preferably, these should express some aspect of the wearer's personality or reflect some of his interests.

Finishing

1. Finish by stitching all around the edge of the yoke with either a blanket stitch or herringbone stitch. Work both fairly closely.

Matching Cuffs and Hatband

1. A dressier effect is obtained when the cuffs are also worked.
2. Make a matching hatband for his favorite hat — a stetson, a straw hat, etc.
3. Measure the circumference of the hat and add 2" (5 cm).
4. Cut the foundation fabric this length and 2" (5 cm) wide.
5. Lay out your scraps as above and embellish as above.
6. Back the band with a piece of grosgrain ribbon and finish like the bookmark on page 170.
7. Fit the band on the hat and mark the spot where a small piece of velcro should be sewn, then sew on the velcro to hold the band in place.

Man's Silk Crazy Patchwork Vest

This easy-to-make silk vest is absolutely elegant for the gentleman in your life. He'll wear it to the theatre, the opera, the concert series, or simply for evening entertaining at home. Your choice of colors, patterns, and thread can make a subtle, rich garment or a bright, colorful, and sure-to-be noticed vest. The vest is not padded.

Technique Used   Traditional

Techniques Suitable   Traditional or semi-traditional

Materials Required

1 yd (1 m) 45" (112.5 cm) wide foundation material
2 yds (2 m) 45" (112.5 cm) wide black lining material or black silk (polyester silk is suitable) of good quality (Any dark, rich color such as burgundy, royal or midnight blue, bottle green, or chocolate brown will look fine but black is the most versatile.)
Scraps of silk in rich, deep colors (Tie silks are excellent combined with dress silks and some plain silks in black, brown, navy, royal blue, rust, gold, bottle green, burgundy, plum, or maroon. Patches should be no bigger than 3" x 3" or 7.5 cm x 7.5 cm as larger pieces will not give the same luxurious effect.)
1 ball black #8 pearl cotton
1 spool black sewing thread
1 spool black buttonhole thread
5 black or brass buttons

Pattern Making

1. Draft the pattern using the sketch given (A) and the pattern-making techniques discussed on page 46 or purchase a commercial pattern in the correct chest size. Look for a pattern with a side panel for easier fitting. This will do away with working the patchwork in the underarm area where it will wear poorly.

Cutting

1. You may cut out the two front pieces in the foundation material or better, trace the shapes onto the foundation material but do not cut out until the pieces are embellished. Then retrace the front vest pieces and cut them out so that the size is still correct.
2. Cut out two linings for the fronts, two backs, and two panels for each side.

Laying Out

1. On the foundation material lay out the scraps, trimming the pieces for

interest. Work on both sides at once in order to balance the colors. *Do not use the same colors and materials in exactly the same places* but try to use each color at least three times on each front and include plain materials for emphasis and contrast.

Pinning and Basting

1. When the pieces are laid out attractively, pin, then baste in place, underlapping and overlapping as necessary and turning under the raw edges.

Embellishment

1. Embroider over the joins, being sure to catch both sides of the patch, and to sew through the foundation material.

2. Stitches used in this vest include single, double, and triple featherstitch; zigzag and plain chain; broad, cable, and alternate chain; open cretan stitch; detached and attached fly stitches; fern stitch and blanket stitch variations; as well as herringbone and cross-stitches.

3. Stitch combinations used are masculine in feeling such as blanket stitch combinations I, II, and V; herringbone stitch combinations I, II, V, VI.

4. Embroidered motifs for the plain patches should also have a masculine feeling. Use nautical motifs, hunting and fishing motifs (animals, fish, birds), initials, "number one" ribbon, automobiles, and leaves. All of the motifs should have some personal significance for the owner of the vest. Consider such symbols as the Masonic logo, service club symbols, and fellowship orders. Be sure that such motifs are in keeping with the scale of the work — they should be small and subtle.

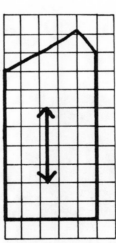

Side panels

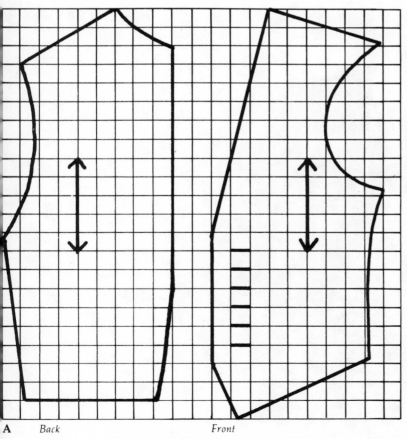

A *Back* *Front*

1 square = 1" (2.5 cm) *Add 5/8" (1.5 cm) seam allowances.*

B

Making Up

1. Press the completed fronts, face down, on a turkish towel.
2. Redraw the front pattern pieces, run a line of machine stitching inside the seam allowance to prevent fraying of stitches or material, then cut out.
3. Sew the side panels of black silk to each of the fronts and press seams.
4. Sew shoulder seams of the back and vest fronts and press.
5. Repeat, sewing side panels to fronts of lining and press seams.
6. Sew shoulder seams of the lining.
7. Insert the lining into the vest using either of the two methods of "Lining a Vest" discussed on pages 61, 62.

Finishing

1. This vest looks best when buttoned so check buttonhole and button placement and mark with pins and basting.
2. Work buttonholes by hand, using black silk buttonhole thread.
3. Sew on black or brass buttons (B).

Note: An easier way to cope with closures is to sew buttons in place but use velcro dots and velcro glue for the actual closure.

Men's or Boys' Casual Crazy Patchwork Vest

Denim (traditional blue or trendy color) or cotton gabardine (in any color he chooses) make this cheerful and comfortable casual vest for men and boys a hands-down favorite. Unpadded, it can be his most useful year-around accessory. Size shown is 38-40. Add a matching crazy patchwork hatband for his stetson to complete the ensemble.

Technique Used   Semi-traditional

Techniques Suitable   Traditional, all semi-traditional methods, and modern machine method

Materials Required

2 yds (2 m) 45" wide (112.5 cm) brushed denim or cotton gabardine
Scraps of cotton ginghams, prints and plains in cotton, and cotton/polyester blends in brown, gold, beige, and blue
1 ball each dark brown and medium blue #8 pearl cotton
1 spool brown sewing thread

Pattern Making

Using the sketch provided (A) and the pattern-making techniques on page 46 draft the pattern pieces for the front, the back, and the front and back yokes. Add 1/2" (1.25 cm) seam allowance, for double seams.

Cutting

1. Cut out two front yoke pieces and one back yoke piece.
2. Measure a length of fabric for fringe the width of your fabric (cross-grained) 45" (112.5 cm) and 4" (10 cm) wide. *Note:* Directions for the fringe are given here but fringe is not shown on the photograph.

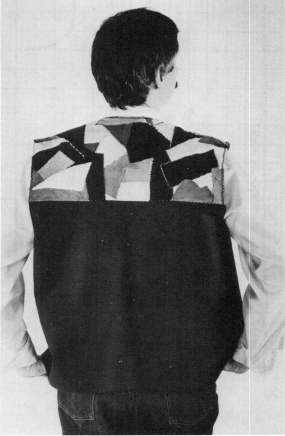

3. Draw a line 1/2" (1.25 cm) in from one edge.

4. Cut the fringe 1/4" (0.6 cm) wide all along the width of the material (B).

5. Run the fringe piece through the washing machine on gentle cycle and let it dry flat to give it that fringed and frayed appearance.

Laying Out

1. Arrange the scraps of material in a pleasing order on the yoke pieces, front and back.

2. Work on all three at the same time, using each color at least three times on each piece, not necessarily in the same place.

3. Use the semi-traditional method of piecing found on page 16.

4. When piecing is completed, press the patchwork.

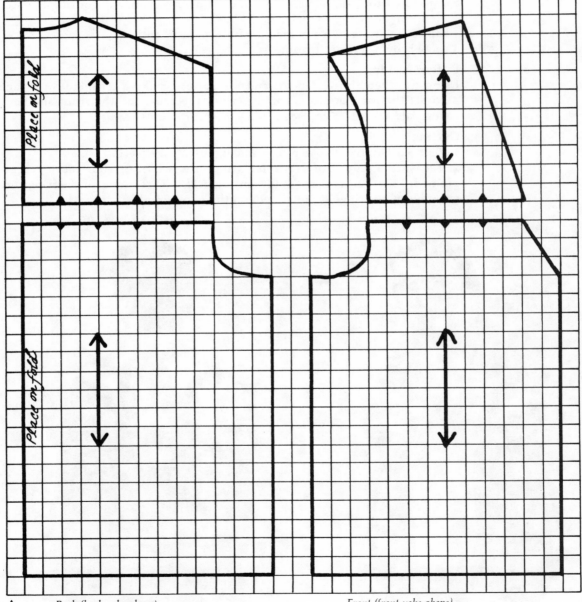

A   *Back (back yoke above)*   *Front (front yoke above)*
     1 square = 1" (2.5 cm)   *Seam allowances included*
                    For double seams add 1/2" (1.25 cm)

Embellishment

1. Stitches used on the vest should be simple to give a masculine look. Embroidered motifs should also be masculine and casual and reflect the personal interests of the wearer. Nautical motifs on a red, white, and blue vest; cattle brands on a brown, beige, and gold vest; dogs, horses, ducks, fish, and game are all suitable. Because I used only Ultrasuede™ scraps for this garment and the resulting bulk of the overlapping and underlapping was difficult to sew through by hand, I chose to do the embellishment with decorative machine stitches.

Making Up

1. Pin the seam allowances (straight end) of the fringe (if used) to the back and the front pieces of the vest; baste in place.
2. Pin the embellished yoke pieces in place, right sides together, enclosing the seam allowances of the fringe, and machine sew.
3. Sew the side and shoulder seams using a double or french seam (see instructions on pages 54, 55).

Finishing

1. Turn under the raw edges of the armhole and the outer edges of the vest and machine sew a narrow seam; turn again 1/4" (0.6 cm) and machine sew.
2. An alternative method is to finish the raw edges with matching or contrasting bias binding (see instructions on page 57). If you use this method, add an additional 1/2 yd (45 cm) of whichever material you plan to use for the bias binding.
3. Fringe is optional. (For application see General Information, Fringe, pages 48-49.)

Note: If you use Ultrasuede™ for the patches as I did in the model shown, you will find that the suede and the denim are very heavy together and make bulky seams. I finished the neck and armhole seams before I sewed the scraps onto the yoke. Then I sewed the side seams and finished the front and bottom of the vest by turning under 1/2" (1.25 cm) seams twice and then top stitching.

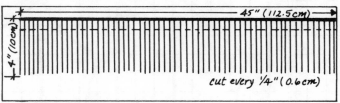

45" (112.5 cm)

4" (10 cm)

cut every 1/4" (0.6 cm)

Optional fringes on pages 48-49.

B   *For denim fringe*

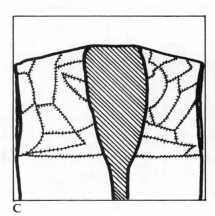
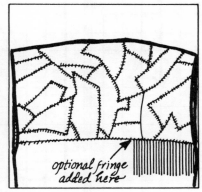

optional fringe added here

C

CHILDREN'S WEAR
Christening Set

If you have a special baby in your life this white-on-white crazy patchwork-trimmed christening dress and bonnet will become your family's heirloom. The dress is made of hand-washable polyester crepe in white and the yoke and bonnet brim are crazy patchwork in novelty-patterned compatible materials. The set is designed for ease in making and comfort for baby, as well as style to make baby (boy or girl) look special.

Technique Used   Traditional

Techniques Suitable   Semi-traditional and modern machine method

Materials Required

2 yds (2 m) 45" (112.5 cm) wide polyester crepe (Any white, easily drapable, hand-washable material would be suitable.)

Scraps of white novelty materials such as eyelet, white cotton brocade, white cotton novelty weave, or white polyester novelty weave (Since this outfit will be washed infrequently and with great care, the usual precautions about washability of all the components can be *relaxed* but not ignored.)

1 ball white #8 pearl cotton or any white embroidery thread with a sheen such as white rayon threads and white silk threads of sufficient weight

5 yds (5 m) of white, washable lace

5 yds (5 m) of 1/2" (1.25 cm) wide white baby satin ribbon

1/4 yd (22.5 cm) soft narrow elastic for the sleeves

4 small snap fasteners or 4 small velcro dots in white

Pattern Making

1. Using the scaled drawings given (A, B) and the pattern-making techniques on page 46, draft the pattern pieces.

2. The size given is for three to four months. For changes in size, see page 47.

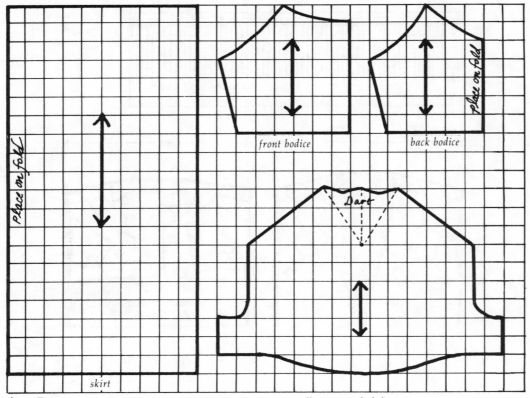

front bodice   back bodice   *Dart*   *sleeve*

Place on fold   *skirt*   *Place on fold*

A   Dress   **1 square = 1" (2.5 cm)**   *Seam allowance included*

Cutting
1. Cut two sleeves, two bodice fronts, two back yokes, one skirt.
2. Cut two bonnet shapes in crepe.
3. Cut the brim portion of the bonnet in fusible interfacing.

Laying Out
1. Fuse one bodice front to interfacing, following the manufacturer's directions.
2. Lay out small scraps, about 2" x 2" (5 cm x 5 cm) in a pleasing design.
3. Pin and then baste in place, overlapping and underlapping as necessary and turning under the raw edges.
4. Repeat with the brim shape.

Embellishment
1. All stitches should be small and dainty in scale. Stitches used in the model shown are single, double, and triple featherstitch; herringbone stitch; plain and zigzag stitch; attached and detached fly stitch; french knots; open cretan stitch; cross-stitch (especially cross-stitch flower); star stitch; satin stitch; and flat stitch. Stitch combinations will likely be too heavy for such a dainty garment. Tiny stitch motifs may be used on a very plain piece. Choose very small designs of flowers, leaves, trailing ribbons, tiny birds, and butterflies.

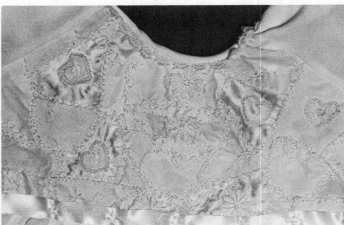

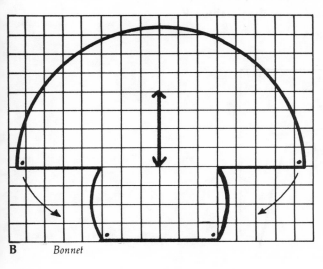

B   *Bonnet*

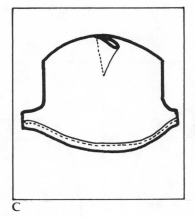

C

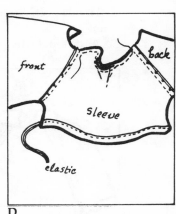

D

Making Up
Dress

1. Use french seams (see page 54) wherever possible or machine overcast seams.

2. Stitch 1/4" (0.6 cm) hem (turned under) on the lower edge of the sleeve for the elastic.

3. Stitch in the tuck at the top of the sleeves.

4. Fold and baste across the upper edge (C).

5. With right sides together, stitch the sleeves to the armhole edges of the bodice front and back (D). Clip curves.

6. Cut two pieces of elastic the size of the baby's wrist measurement plus 1/2" (1.25 cm).

7. On the inside, thread elastic through casing and secure.

8. Stitch underarm seam from waist to wrist on each side (E).

9. Apply ribbon and lace to skirt (G).

10. Gather the upper edge of the skirt by hand or machine (F).

11. Machine stitch to 6" (15 cm) from top.

12. With right sides together, pin skirt to bodice, matching centre fronts and back opening.

13. Machine stitch and press the seam *up*.

14. Turn under the raw edges of the skirt and neckline in a narrow double seam. Hand stitch. Alternatively, make narrow bias binding from the crepe and bind (see page 57.)

15. Machine sew narrow lace over hem.

16. Turn under the raw edges of the back with a narrow double hem and hand or machine stitch. Again, you may choose to bind these edges.

17. Lap over about 1" (2.5 cm) and fasten with white velcro or snaps at neck and waist.

Finishing

1. On the outside of the waistline, tack the narrow ribbon and/or lace.

2. Secure with french knots.

3. Edge the neckline with narrow lace.

4. Edge the hemline (turned up in a narrow hem, twice) with lace.

5. You may choose to make a narrow band of the crazy patchwork trim and stitch it to the skirt (before gathering) about 2" (5 cm) above the lower edge.

6. Hand stitch narrow white satin ribbon over the raw edges of the patchwork trim.

7. Additional rows of lace may be added.

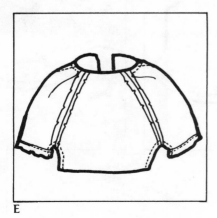

E

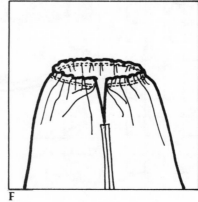

F

Making Up

Bonnet

1. Using diagram B as your guide, bring together the seamlines of the back raw edges and stitch (H).

2. Repeat with the lining.

3. With right sides together, stitch lining and bonnet together, matching seams and leaving a small opening at centre back to turn (I).

4. Turn and press.

5. Attach lace edging and ribbon to cover raw edges of lace edging around the brim of the bonnet, neatly fastening it off at the back.

Finishing

1. Attach ribbon ties (J).

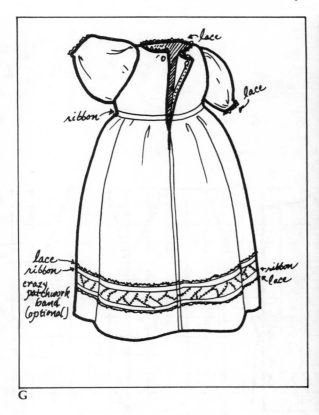

G

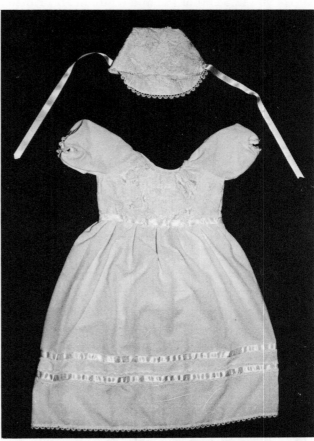

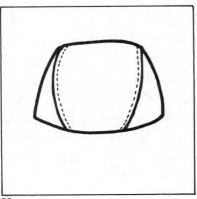

H

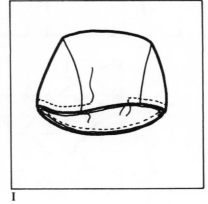

I

J

"Little Sweetheart" Toddlers'
Crazy Patchwork Jacket and Hat

Imagine your own little sweetheart in this darling jacket. All of the five prints used have red and white hearts on them. The prints are combined with white eyelet and red stitching for a valentine-heart jacket that's perfect for any day of the year. The size shown is for a toddler, size 3.

Technique Used   Semi-traditional with variation I

Techniques Suitable   All

Materials Required

1-1/2 yds (1.5 m) red brushed denim 45" (112.5 cm) wide

1-1/2 yds (1.5 m) bonded quilt batting

1/4 yd (22.5 cm) of red and white heart prints (The model shown has three red-background prints and two white-background prints.)

1/4 yd (22.5 cm) white eyelet material

1 spool red sewing thread

1 spool red #8 pearl cotton

1/2 yd (45 cm) of one of the red-background prints for bias binding

Pattern Making

1. Using the directions in the pattern-making section draw the pattern pieces for the jacket (front, back, arms) (A) and the hat (crown sections and brim) (B). Or purchase a commercial pattern with raglan sleeves for the jacket — the fewer seams the better.

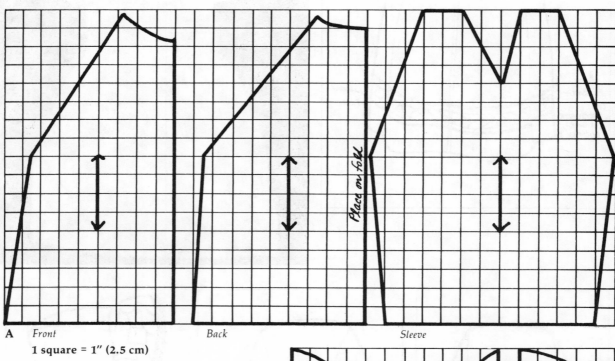

A   Front   Back   Sleeve

1 square = 1" (2.5 cm)

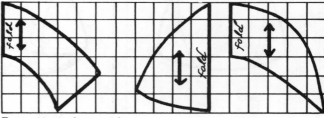

B   *Hat for boy or girl*

Jacket
Cutting

1. Lay out the pattern pieces on the brushed red denim, being sure that the right side of the denim will be on the inside of the jacket. (That means that you place the pattern pieces on the wrong side of the material.)
2. Cut two jacket fronts, one back, and two sleeves, using the red denim.
3. Cut the same number of pieces using batting.

Laying Out

1. With the front piece before you, brushed side *down* and corresponding batting piece on top, pin in several places.
2. Starting at the left top side, place the pieces in your chosen order (refer to directions for semi-traditional method on page 16).
3. Sew around each pattern piece by machine before trimming edges.

Embellishment

1. On each pattern piece, because of the angularity of the crazy patchwork pieces, applique a heart in plain red by hand or use your sewing machine. Keep your stitches fairly simple on this project to suit the juvenile style. Use single, double, and triple featherstitch; cross-stitch; herringbone stitch; attached and detached chain stitch; zigzag; straight, flat stitch; french knots; star stitch; outline; and backstitch for little embroidered motifs. *Be careful not to stitch through to the red denim.*
2. Not every seam needs to be covered with stitchery.

Making Up

1. Use a 5/8" (1.5 cm) seam which has been allowed for in the pattern.
2. Sew the sleeve slash which gives shape to the sleeve.
3. Make up some bias binding for the edges (see directions on page 57).
4. Trim the seams.
5. Open the bias binding and iron the raw edges under on one side.
6. Apply the binding by hand (if you don't want it to show on the front) or by machine (if it doesn't matter to you that it will show). If you take care with this the jacket can be used on the reverse side.
7. Attach the fronts and back to the sleeve pieces and cover the seams in the same way.

8. With double-fold bias binding, start at the centre back neck and sew by machine to the raw edges of the jacket and continue all around until you come to the centre back neck edge. Fold back the ends of the binding at the start and the finish or overlap.

9. Apply the binding to the raw edges of the sleeves in the same way.

Finishing

1. The way I like to finish the binding is to fold it to the back and hand stitch it in place making sure the stitches are invisible.

2. However, if you want to use the "stitch-in-the-ditch" method, refer to directions on page 45.

3. Hand embroider the child's name on an applique heart on the left side over her heart.

4. Close with ties made from the bias binding. Each tie should be 12" (30 cm) long.

Hat
Cutting

1. Lay out the pattern pieces on the brushed red denim. Be sure that the right side of the denim is on the *inside* for the brim or bill and on the *outside* for the crown (which is unquilted).

2. Cut four crown sections and two brim sections.

3. Cut two brim sections from bonded quilt batting.

Laying Out

1. On each brim piece (brushed side *down*) with batting on top, place the pieces in your chosen order, seaming each down in the "pressed-piecing" technique as described in the instructions on page 16.

2. Use each of your five prints and eyelet at least once on each brim piece, keeping the scale of the pieces smaller than that used on the jacket.

Embellishment

1. On such small pattern pieces it is impossible to add applique pieces, so sew down those seams that were left to be done by hand, using red #8 pearl cotton and a variety of simple embroidery stitches. Do not take the stitches through to the red denim.

Making Up

1. Seam the crown pieces together by machine in pairs.

2. Then seam together two pair, and finally both halves.

3. Overcast the seam allowance and press open.

4. Seam together the brim pieces by machine; trim closely.

5. Open out some seam binding and hand stitch it over the seams so it doesn't show through to the upper part of the brim.

6. Attach the brim to the crown, hand baste, and adjust for fit.

7. Machine sew, then trim seams.

Finishing

1. Try the hat on the child and mark the position for ties over the ears.

2. Make two ties, each 12" (30 cm) long from bias binding folded again and seamed or see tie closure directions on page 50.

3. Attach in position with sturdy hand sewing.

4. Cover the seam with opened-out seam binding applied as described above.

5. With double-fold seam binding, cover the raw edges of the brim; sew down the raw edges of the binding to the raw edges of the brim.

6. Hand sew or "stitch-in-the-ditch" with machine sewing to anchor down the folded edge side.

"Lambie Pie" Crazy Patchwork Baby Quilt and Pillow

"Lambie Pie" will certainly be the favorite of your favorite baby. The medley of pastel colors combined with yellow as the background material make it suitable for either a boy or a girl. The matching pillow is quickly and easily made.

Technique Used   Semi-traditional with variation I

Techniques Suitable   Traditional, semi-traditional with variations I or II

Materials Required

3 yds (3 m) yellow and white gingham small check for backing and picot edge
1 yd (1 m) plain yellow for centre
1/2 yd (45 cm) white eyelet for lamb and border
Assorted scraps of pastel cottons and cotton/polyester blends in pink, blue, orange, mauve, green, yellow, and turquoise — about 1/8 yd (11.35 cm) for the border, including enough pink and blue for the face, ears, and legs of the lamb
2 yds (2 m) bonded quilt batting (polyester)
1/2 package unbonded quilt batting for stuffing pillow
1 ball yellow #8 pearl cotton for embroidery and tying the quilt
Yellow sewing or quilting thread
1 skein dark blue embroidery thread — stranded or pearl
100 small gold safety pins

Pattern Making

1. Draw the lamb pattern. Remember to add 1/4" (0.6 cm) seam allowance.
2. Draw out the quilting motifs of barn, house, fence, and field (pattern is one-half actual size) (A).

Cutting

1. Cut a square of plain yellow 28" x 28" (70 cm x 70 cm).
2. Fold in half twice on the diagonal and press in the folds as a guide for placement of the lamb and the quilting motifs (B).

3. Cut the leg and two outer ear pieces from the pale blue scraps.

4. Cut the face and two inner ears from pink. Mark in the features of the face.

5. Cut the body of the lamb as well as the head from eyelet.

6. Cut two quilt foundation pieces 28″ x 6″ (70 cm x 15 cm) and two border foundation pieces 34″ x 6″ (85 cm x 15 cm).

7. Cut two bonded quilt batt pieces in each of the sizes given above.

Laying Out

1. Baste under the seam allowance on the lamb pieces and press.

2. Embroider features in dark blue.

3. Pin the lamb in place in the centre of the yellow square.

Lamb   1 square = 1″ (2.5 cm)

B

A   Quilt design motifs

1 square = 1/2″ (1.25 cm)

Border

1. Select a color order (e.g., mauve, white eyelet, yellow, turquoise, pink, green, orange, and then repeat).

2. Using the semi-traditional method with variation I described on page 17, machine sew down the scraps. Keep in mind the value of appliqueing curved shapes to break up the angular lines which result from this method of piecing.

Embellishment

1. You may choose to embellish all the seamlines or only about one-third of them.

2. Using the yellow #8 pearl cotton embroidery thread, work the following stitches and combinations: fern stitch; open cretan; open cretan with fly stitch; herringbone plain and herringbone with fly stitch; detached fly stitch; plain and zigzag chain stitch; chain stitch with upright detached chain; detached chain in triple petal motif; single, double, and triple featherstitch; star stitch; detached cross-stitch; and combination stitches.

Making Up

1. Using an applique stitch sew down the lamb.

2. Using an HB pencil (very hard lead) lightly trace the quilting motifs in each corner of the yellow centre piece, about 6" (15 cm) from edge.

3. Sew the two short side pieces of the border to the yellow centre piece by machine.

4. Add the longer borders (C).

5. Press.

6. Using the top as a guide, cut a piece of bonded quilt batting and a piece of yellow gingham (backing).

7. Sandwich the batting between the top and the lining. Lay out carefully on a flat surface and be sure there are no wrinkles.

8. Using small gold safety pins, start at the centre and work outwards, pinning all layers together about every 4" (10 cm).

9. Hand or machine quilt around the lamb and the barn, fence, field, and house motifs.

10. Hand or machine quilt "in-the-ditch" along the seamline joining the centre and border strip.

11. Using the same yellow #8 pearl cotton embroidery thread, tie inconspicuously about every 4" (10 cm) along the border strip to hold the three layers together.

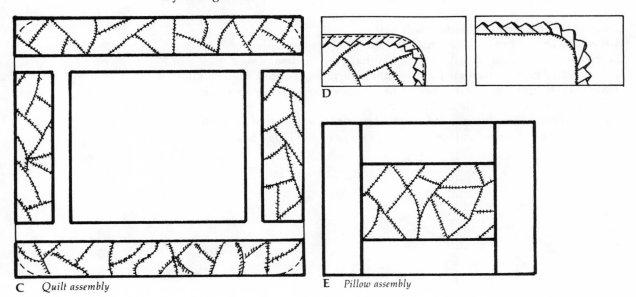

C   *Quilt assembly*   D   E   *Pillow assembly*

Finishing

1. Using a saucer as your guide, gently round off corners of the quilt (C).
2. Make one hundred 3" (7.5 cm) picots (see page 60).
3. Sew them together in one long strip by machine.
4. By machine, sew the picot strip, face down, to the *top only* (pin the batting and backing out of the way) (D).
5. By hand, turn under the gingham backing and sew to the picots. Be sure *not* to go right through to the front.

PILLOW

1. Using the semi-traditional method with variation I piece larger scraps about 5" x 5" (12.5 cm x 12.5 cm) into a rectangle 12" x 9" (30 cm x 22.5 cm).
2. Embellish with star stitch; single, double, and triple featherstitch; and blanket stitch.
3. Cut two borders of yellow gingham 12" x 2-1/2" (30 cm x 6.25 cm) and sew them to the top and bottom rectangles.
4. Cut two borders of yellow gingham 14" x 2-1/2" (35.5 cm x 6.25 cm) and sew to the ends of the rectangle.
5. Press well.
6. Using the top as a guide, cut a backing of yellow gingham.
7. With right sides together, sew around all four sides, leaving a space to turn.
8. Clip corners and turn, poking out corners.
9. Press.
10. Stuff with handfulls of unbonded batting, being sure to get the batting well into the corners.
11. Sew opening closed with small overcast stitches using yellow sewing thread.

Three-Piece Baby Feeding Set

A welcome change from the traditional baby quilt as a gift, this set consists of a generous bib, a "burp pad" for Grandpa's shoulder, and a high chair or lap pad that can also be used in a car seat. The set is shown in 1/4" (0.6 cm) yellow and white gingham which makes it suitable for a boy or a girl.

Technique Used   Traditional

Techniques Suitable   Traditional or machine method

Materials Required

3 yds (3 m) 45" (112.5 cm) wide yellow and white gingham for pad, lap pad, and bib

3 yds (3 m) of bonded polyester quilt batt

1/8 yd (11.25 cm) brown and white gingham for the applique

Scraps of pink, turquoise, and yellow gingham for the bear's vest

1/8 yd (11.25 cm) iron-on medium-weight interfacing to back the applique

1/8 yd (11.25 cm) crisp Tear-away or tissue paper to back the applique

2 yds (2 m) material for pleated/ruffled edging

1 spool yellow #8 pearl cotton for embroidery and tying, a bit of pink, blue, and rose pearl or stranded cotton for the features of the teddy bear

1 fabric gluestick
1 spool brown polyester sewing thread if you are appliqueing by machine, or
1 spool medium brown #8 pearl cotton if you are appliqueing by hand

Pattern Making

1. Using the sketch given here, make up the brown paper pattern for the three pieces and cut out. Be sure to allow for seams (A).
2. Draft the teddy bear applique shown and, using the dressmaker's carbon, transfer to the brown and white gingham. Do this *three times.* If you plan to applique by machine it is not necessary to include a seam allowance. None is included in this pattern. If you choose to applique by hand, allow 1/4" (0.6 cm) seam allowance to turn under.
3. For ease in working do *not* cut out pieces until they have been embroidered.

Laying Out

1. Using tiny scraps of gingham, fill in the vest. Baste down each piece as it is laid in place.

Cutting

1. Cut out two pieces each of the lap pad, bib, and burp pad in gingham and one of each shape in quilt batting.

Embellishment

1. Before cutting the three bears out of the brown and white gingham, embroider the seam edges of the crazy patchwork on the vest, using the yellow pearl cotton. Simple stitches used in the photographed sample are double featherstitch, attached fly stitch, zigzag chain, plain chain, and blanket stitch. Finish off by outlining the whole vest in a small-scale blanket stitch.

2. Embroider a rose bowtie in the space under the bear chin.

3. Embroider the blue gingham palms, soles, and ears of the bear in place using a small-scale yellow blanket stitch. Hold the piece in place with fabric gluestick while working.

4. Embroider the bear's cheeks in light pink using an open blanket stitch in a circle, his blue eyes in the same stitch, and his rose muzzle in satin stitch with a neat backstitch worked around the edge when completed.

Making Up

1. Press the completed embroidery.

2. Fuse it to the scrap of medium-weight interfacing to give body to the applique.

3. With sharp scissors, carefully cut out the three appliques.

4. Position them as shown in the photograph and pin in place.

5. On the wrong side of the gingham, pin the crisp Tear-away™ or two layers of tissue paper.

6. Set your sewing machine for "satin stitch," load with brown sewing thread.

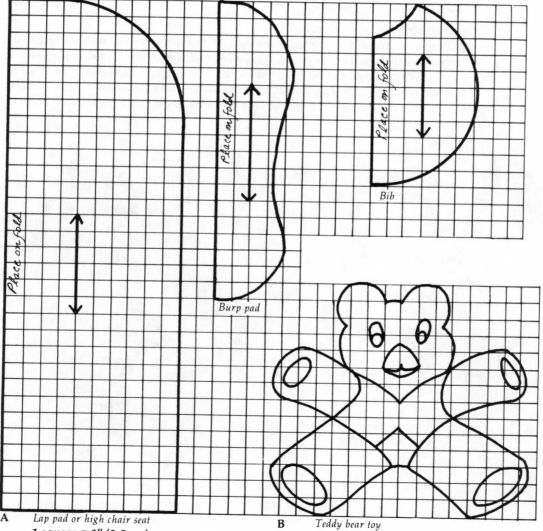

A   *Lap pad or high chair seat*
1 square = 1" (2.5 cm)

B   *Teddy bear toy*
1 square = 1" (2.5 cm)
For applique 1 square = 1/2" (1.25 cm)

7. Machine sew the appliques in place.

8. If you omit the Tear-away backing, then baste under the seam allowance. Pin the applique in place and, using brown pearl embroidery cotton or stranded cotton, use a fairly close, small blanket stitch to applique bears in place.

9. Measure around the bib, burp pad, and chair pad; double this figure for the length of the ruffling you need to make.

10. Cut this length 4" (10 cm) wide (you will have to piece it). Join to make one long strip.

11. Press in half.

12. If you have a machine ruffler you can make the edging in about fifteen minutes.

13. If ruffling without this accessory, thread your machine with quilting thread for strength, and using the largest stitch, make the ruffles in six or eight sections.

14. Adjust the ruffles so they are even; then using a stitch length of 10, sew over them to stabilize them while you work. Clip the thread ends.

Finishing

Lap Pad

1. Make a "textile sandwich" of gingham, batting, and embellished top, right side up.

2. Pin in place with small gold safety pins.

3. If you wish, hand or machine quilt around the teddy bear motif.

4. Using a double strand of the yellow pearl cotton tie at 4" (10 cm) intervals and clip the tuft closely.

5. An alternative method is to machine quilt along the gingham lines. If you choose to do this, stop and start your quilting 1" (2.5 cm) in from the edge. You will need this allowance when attaching the edging.

6. Pin the raw edge of the edging to the raw edge of the top of the pad. Holding the batting and backing out of your way, machine stitch down. Double-fold your raw edge at the beginning and ending and start half-way down the longest side for an inconspicuous join.

7. Spread the pad out on a flat surface, right side down.

8. Straighten the edges and fold under the raw edge of the backing and slip stitch (using either white or yellow thread) by hand so that no stitches come through to the right side.

Burp Pad

1. Assemble and finish it in the same way as lap pad.

Bib

1. Assemble and finish in the same way but do not put a ruffle around the inner neck edge. Instead, cut a length of bias in the same material as the ruffle 20" (50 cm) long and 2" (5 cm) wide. Press in half lengthwise.

2. Place raw edges of the bias binding to the raw edge of the inner neck, pin at the centre front and then to each side.

3. Machine sew down.

4. Turn the raw edges in and machine sew the tie ends neatly.

Teddy Bear Crib Toy With Crazy Patchwork Vest

Babies love soft toys they can hold in their hands. This teddy bear matches the three-piece feeding set or can be a lovely gift on its own.

Technique Used   Traditional

Techniques Suitable   Traditional, semi-traditional, and machine method

Materials Required
1/2 yd (45 cm) brown and white gingham
Scraps of yellow, blue, turquoise, and pink gingham, plain rose for muzzle
1 spool yellow #8 pearl cotton
Scraps of unbonded quilt batting or polyfil toy stuffing (Bonded batt is too stiff for best results.)
1 spool white sewing thread
Scraps of blue, pink, and rose embroidery thread

Pattern Making
1. Using the pattern-making techniques, make a paper pattern for the front of the bear (B, page 116). Be sure to allow 1/4" (0.6 cm) seam allowance.
2. Trace pattern onto brown and white gingham. Be sure to centre one of the dark rows of checks in the centre of the face.
3. Trace all the features and the vest onto this shape.
4. Trace a second shape but omit all facial and limb details (for back of toy).
5. Trace out muzzle shape on pink cotton.
6. *Do not cut out* until the embroidery and patchwork are completed for ease in working.

Laying Out and Embellishment
1. Lay out and embellish according to the techniques described in the teddy bear applique in the feeding set on pages 115, 116.
2. With a seam ripper cut a small slit in the gingham behind the muzzle.

Cutting
1. Cut out carefully. Be sure to leave a seam allowance.

Making Up
1. Stuff the muzzle lightly and whipstitch the opening closed.
2. With the right sides together, sew on machine (set stitch length at 12).
3. Leave a 2" (5 cm) opening at the side of the head for stuffing and turning.
4. Clip all curved edges.
5. Turn carefully, poking out all curves and seams.
6. Press well.
7. Using a pencil to get the stuffing into all parts of the toy, stuff with small handfulls of polyfil or unbonded quilt batting. Be sure not to overstuff.

Finishing
1. Using white sewing thread, carefully turn in the raw edges of the opening and with a close whipstitch (overcast stitch), sew the opening closed by hand.
2. With yellow pearl cotton embroider over the seams at the side of the vest so the side seams are not visible.

CHRISTMAS PROJECTS

Victorian-Style Christmas Wreath

This elegantly sophisticated wreath will add a festive touch to your holiday decorating. For a true Victorian look choose satins, silks, brocades, plushes, and velvets in ruby red, black, dark brown, dark purple, emerald green, and gold and embellish with gold-colored stitchery. For a no less elegant effect you may wish to pick up the colors in your decorating scheme and combine them with ecru lace and stitching that is darker or lighter than your main color. Finished wreath is 18" (45 cm) in diameter.

Technique Used   Traditional

Techniques Suitable   All

Materials Required

1 yd (1 m) of 42" (105 cm) wide foundation fabric

Scraps of silk, satin, brocade, velvet, lace, and other exotic fabrics in jewel shades, plus dark brown, black, grey, rust, and navy

1 ball gold-colored #5 pearl cotton

1/2 yd (45 cm) dark-colored cotton for the backing

1/2 package polyester quilt batting, unbonded

1 darning needle

1 yd (1 m) satin ribbon in the color of your choice (I used red)

Pattern Making

1. Trace the pattern pieces A and B given here full-size onto cardboard for a template. *Seam allowances are included.*

Cutting

1. Trace eight A and eight B pieces on the foundation material.
2. Cut out.

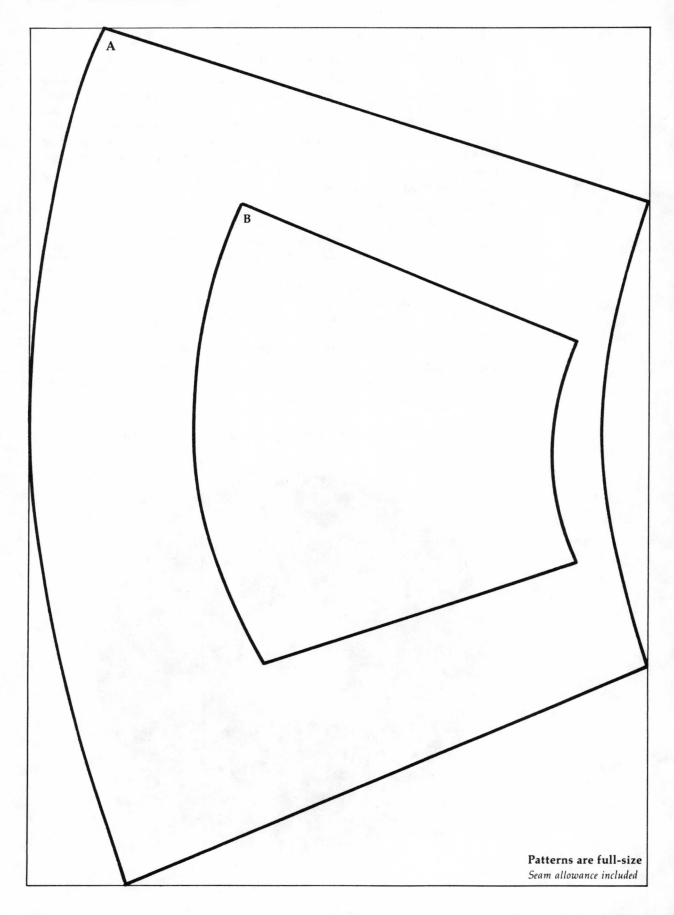

A

B

Patterns are full-size
Seam allowance included

Laying Out

1. Predetermine a color sequence and divide your scraps into color piles.
2. Lay out the sixteen pieces to form a circle and place the scraps on them. Adjust placement of the pieces for a visually pleasing effect; consider the texture of the scraps as well.

Pinning and Basting

1. Underlap heavy materials and overlap lightweight materials and pin.
2. Hand or machine baste in place.

Embellishment

1. Stitches used on the wreath include single, double, and triple featherstitch; open cretan stitch; star stitch; detached and attached fly stitch; sheaf stitch; herringbone stitch; cross-stitch; detached and attached chain stitch; couching; running stitch; flat and straight stitch; french knots. Any variety of combination stitches are also appropriate for this style wreath (see photograph below).

Making Up

1. Join piece A to piece B. Be careful to match the edges and centre of the two pieces and to take an exact 1/2" (1.25 cm) seam throughout (A).
2. Join each pair.
3. Press these seams towards the centre of the wreath.
4. Join these pie-shaped pieces in pairs and press all seams. Match centre seamlines carefully.
5. Join two pair together to make four sections and repeat with the remaining four sections.
6. Join the two resulting pieces together and press the seams to centre of wreath.
7. Embellish the seamlines with a variety of stitches using the same color thread as before.
8. Using the circular wreath as your pattern cut a backing from dark-colored cotton.
9. With right sides of top and backing together, machine sew the outer seam.
10. Clip the curve, turn, and press.
11. Using unbonded quilt batting scraps, carefully stuff the wreath half full.
12. Then, folding the raw edges of the centre of the wreath together and using a very fine whipstitch or overcast stitch in the color of the backing, hand sew this centre seam, completing the stuffing as you go.

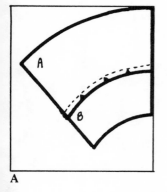

A

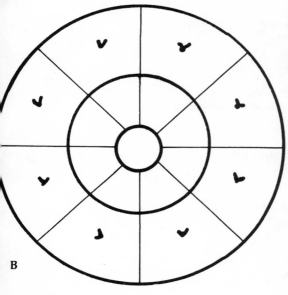

B

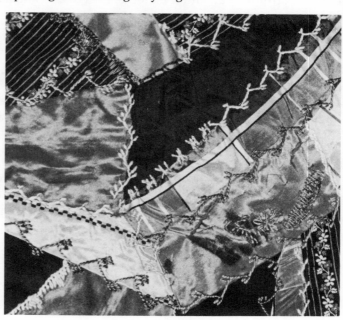

Finishing

1. Using a double strand of the embroidery thread and a darning needle, tie in the centre of each of the eight sections (B). Pull the tie very tightly and tie securely.

2. At the top of the wreath, work a double strand of the embroidery cotton into a hanger. Work over the loop several times with a buttonhole stitch to strengthen.

3. Attach a pre-tied satin ribbon to the top front of the wreath or at the bottom right side.

Note: If you use large scraps of plain colored material in each pie-shaped section, embroider a little Christmas motif in that plain section for added embellishment.

Victorian Crazy Patchwork Christmas Ornaments

These lovely ornaments can be made very quickly. They sell well at bazaars and they are also lovely keepsakes for family members. Use scraps that have some meaning for the recipient and include pieces of lace, etc., for a memento that will become a treasured family heirloom. The ornament pictured was made for my daughter, Sarah. I used the same patches as those for her wedding dress trim and I included tiny lace medallions from *my* wedding dress.

Technique Used   Traditional

Technique Suitable   Traditional

Materials Required

2" (5 cm) diameter silk-covered or glass Christmas ball
1/8 yd (11.35 cm) of foundation material (This amount will provide foundation for at least three ornaments.)
Scraps of materials in silk, satin, velvet, lace, etc., about 2" (5 cm) in diameter
1 spool turquoise or pink #5 pearl cotton
1/8 yd (11.25 cm) of 2" (5 cm) wide satin ribbon
Scrap of dainty lace edging about 10" (25 cm) long
Fabric gluestick
1 package narrow pink baby ribbon

Pattern Making

1. No pattern is required.

Cutting

1. Cut a strip of foundation material 10" (25 cm) long and 2-1/2" (6.25 cm) wide.

Laying Out

1. Lay out your scraps in a pleasing order (A). Pin and baste the scraps to the foundation material.

Embellishment

1. Use rich embellishment and stitch combinations. Include stitches such as single, double, and triple featherstitch; herringbone stitch alone and in combinations; open cretan stitch; zigzag chain; star stitch; french knots. Let your imagination soar and make this a very richly embellished strip.

2. Add lace medallions and over-embroider these (B).

3. Embroider date and initials of maker and/or recipient on plain patch.

Making Up

1. Press, face down, on a turkish towel. Trim edges neatly.

2. Place satin ribbon together with the worked strip, wrong sides together, and pin.

3. Using the sewing machine, sew through both layers.

4. Attach the lace edging to both edges by machine, using matching thread.

5. Turn under raw edges by hand (C).

Finishing

1. Place the patchwork band around the widest part of the silk-covered or glass ball and hold in place with gluestick.

2. Using a fine whipstitch and overlapping the ends of the strip about 1" (2.5 cm), sew the ends of the band together.

3. If using a foam-core ball, tiny pins can be placed at intervals to help secure the band, but the gluestick will usually be sufficient. Make sure the band around the ball is tight.

4. Add a narrow ribbon loop and, if desired, lace, ribbon, and tiny artificial flowers. (I used tiny silk flowers from Sarah's wedding bouquet.)

5. Hand sew a 6" (15 cm) long tassel made of baby ribbon to the bottom of the ball (D, E).

Note: Use tatted or crocheted handmade lace on the edging. It can be stiffened in a sugar and water solution or a thick starch solution. White eyelet edging can be lovely as well. Don't overlook the beauty of pastel silks and satins, moirés and velvets. An all-pastel ball is lovely.

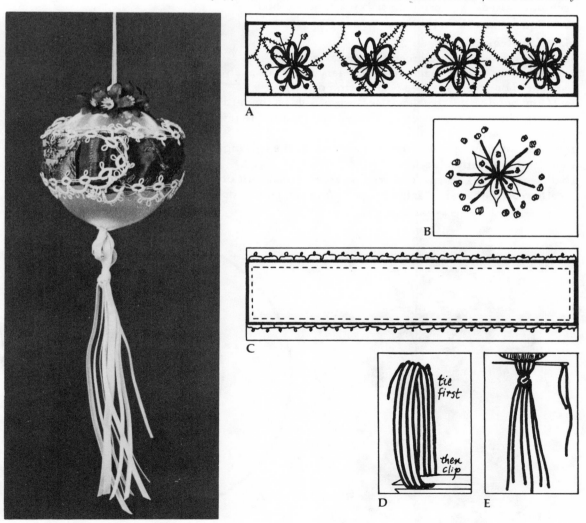

Making the Tassle
1. Cut off 4" of ribbon and set aside.
2. Loop remainder of ribbon as shown (D).
3. Secure by sewing a piece of ribbon around the tassle 1-1/2" (3.75 cm) from the top . Clip bottom loops once tassle is secured by ribbon (D).
4. Hand sew the tassle to the bottom of the ball (E).

"Country" Victorian Christmas Set

A variety of Christmas-type red, green, and white prints, machine-pieced and covered with machine embroidery can create the "look" of country Victorian with very little effort. Set consists of crazy patchwork Christmas tree skirt, crazy patchwork wreath, crazy patchwork Christmas stocking, and crazy patchwork Christmas tree ornaments.

Crazy Patchwork Christmas Tree Skirt

This Christmas tree skirt is so easily made you'll want to make extras for your group's bazaar or for gifts.

Technique Used   Modern materials machine method

Techniques Suitable   All

Materials Required
Scraps of red, white, and green Christmas prints
Red and green sewing machine embroidery thread or plain sewing thread
1 spool red or green #5 or #8 pearl cotton or yarn
1 yd (1 m) bonded quilt batting (Use the type sold by the yard or metre which is usually the least expensive. It is heavily bonded and that is a good attribute for this project.)
1 yd (1 m) of either plain green or plain red for the backing
1 yd (1 m) foundation fabric
1 yd (1 m) 45" (112.5 cm) wide red or green broadcloth or 3 yds (3 m) pre-gathered white eyelet edging for picot (prairie) points (optional)

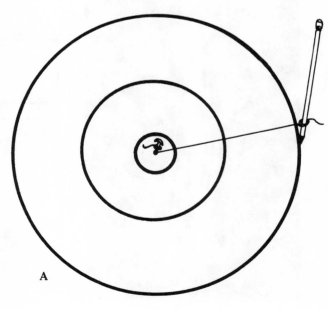

A

Pattern Making

1. Decide the diameter of the skirt you wish to make. A good size is 36" (90 cm) in diameter.
2. Using a double sheet of newspaper and a string 18" (45 cm) long tied to a sharp pencil, draw a circle (A).
3. Shorten the string to 9" (22.5 cm) and draw another circle inside the first. Use the same central point (A).
4. Shorten the string again to 3" (7.5 cm) and draw a third circle in the centre. Use the same central point (A).
5. Cut out around the large circle.
6. Fold the circle in four and crease.
7. Cut out the centre of the smallest circle and discard the cut out piece.
8. Cut along the creases you have made.
9. Cut along the perimeter of the second circle. This will give you four small pie shaped pieces X and four larger curved pieces Y (B).
10. Use one set as your patterns. Be sure to add seam allowances.

Cutting

1. Cut out four foundation pieces using pattern piece X and four foundation pieces using pattern piece Y.
2. Cut four X and four Y lining pieces.

Laying Out

1. It is not necessary to plan this type of patchwork beforehand. Using your decorative machine stitches (or satin stitch), turn under the raw edges of the patches and underlap and overlap as necessary. You may want to arrange your piles of patches by color and use them in a preplanned sequence, (see planned crazy patchwork instructions on page 18).
2. Sew the scraps to the foundation.

Making Up

1. Machine sew pattern pieces X to pattern pieces Y. Be sure to preserve the curved seam.
2. Clip at frequent intervals and press towards Y.
3. Sew two X/Y units together, then add one unit on each side, leaving one seam unsewn for turning (C) and for putting skirt around the tree.
4. Press.
5. Go over these seams with decorative machine stitching.
6. Cut out four stars and a yoke piece from crazy patchwork yardage and machine applique in place.

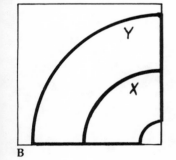

B

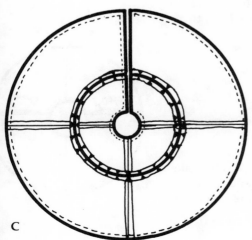

C

Finishing

The tree skirt in the photograph shows white eyelet ruffle edging. See the section on ruffles or if you prefer picot edging turn to these instructions on page 60.

1. Once you have chosen your edging and have it made, assemble with the tree skirt, face up on the bottom with the eyelet or the edging facing inward.
Top this with the lining face down on the skirt, and then the batting, if used. Pin carefully.

2. Machine sew through all layers, leaving one edge open for turning.

3. Trim and clip seams.

4. Turn, press lightly if desired.

5. Hand stitch the opening closed with matching thread.

6. Using yarn or embroidery cotton, tie the skirt together.

Note: This pattern can be used to create an elegant silk and velvet Victorian tree skirt as well. Try it in pastels for a delicate look.

Crazy Patchwork Wreath

This wreath makes a festive addition to the other "country" Victorian pieces in the Christmas ensemble. Use the pattern and directions given for the Victorian wreath.

Technique Used   Modern materials machine method

Techniques Suitable   All

Materials Required

1 yd (1 m) green or red broadcloth for backing
1 yd (1 m) foundation material (as for tree skirt)
1 bag polyfil stuffing
1 yd (1 m) red or green broadcloth for optional prairie or picot points
Scraps of red, green, and white Christmas prints about 3" x 3" (7.5 cm x 7.5 cm)
Red and green sewing or machine embroidery thread
Red or green #5 or #8 pearl cotton for tying
1 yd (1 m) red or green broadcloth for optional prairie or picot points

Pattern Making

1. Copy full-sized pattern given for piece A and piece B on page 120.

Cutting

1. Follow the directions given for the Victorian wreath.

Making Up

1. Use the modern materials machine method with satin stitch or machine decorative stitching, underlapping or overlapping pieces as required and turning edges under.

Embellishments

Machine decorative stitching can be put on all patches and seams.

Finishing

1. Assemble as for Victorian wreath.

2. Before sewing top and backing together, make picot (prairie) points if desired and sew to outer edge of the wreath.

3. Complete assembly as for Victorian wreath.

4. A stitching enthusiast, Joyce Netzke's simplified stuffing trick is to make the back in two parts. Sew both inner seamline and outer seamline leaving seamlines X open (A). Stuff through here. Then hand or machine sew these seams shut.

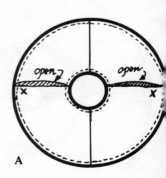

A

Crazy Patchwork Stocking

The generous size of this Christmas stocking will make it a favorite with the lucky owner. The machine techniques used make it a fast project, but one lovely enough to hang up year after year.

Technique Used Modern materials machine method

Techniques Suitable All, with modifications

Materials Required

2 yds (2 m) foundation material

1/2 yd (45 cm) pre-gathered eyelet edging for top edge

1 yd (1 m) bonded quilt batting

12" (30 cm) red or green ribbon for loop for hanging or use scraps of the broadcloth

Scraps of red, green, and white Christmas prints, white eyelet, and plain red and green cotton or cotton/polyester blend broadcloth

1 yd (1 m) either red or green broadcloth for lining

1 spool each red and green sewing thread

Pattern Making

1. Using the scaled-up sketch (A), make a paper pattern (1/2" or 1.25 cm seams are allowed).

Cutting

1. Cut out three stocking shapes in the lining material: two for actual lining and one for back of stocking.
2. Cut two shapes from the batting.
3. Cut one shape from pre-worked patchwork.

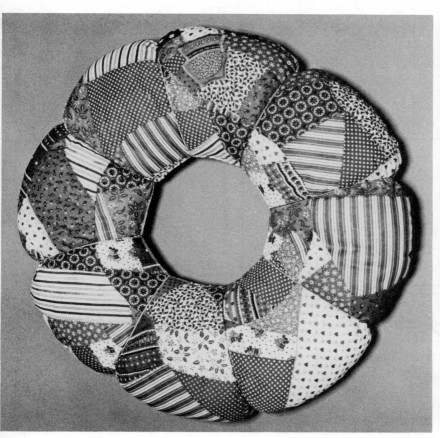

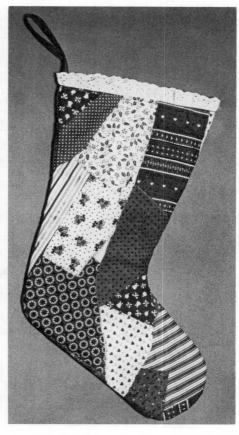

4. Place the lining, right side down, on the table.

5. Cover with the quilt batting shape. Pin or baste well.

Laying Out

1. Organize your prints by color in separate piles. Determine a sequence.

Making Up

1. Refer to machine methods on page 17. Starting at one corner of the stocking turn under raw edges, overlapping and underlapping as necessary.

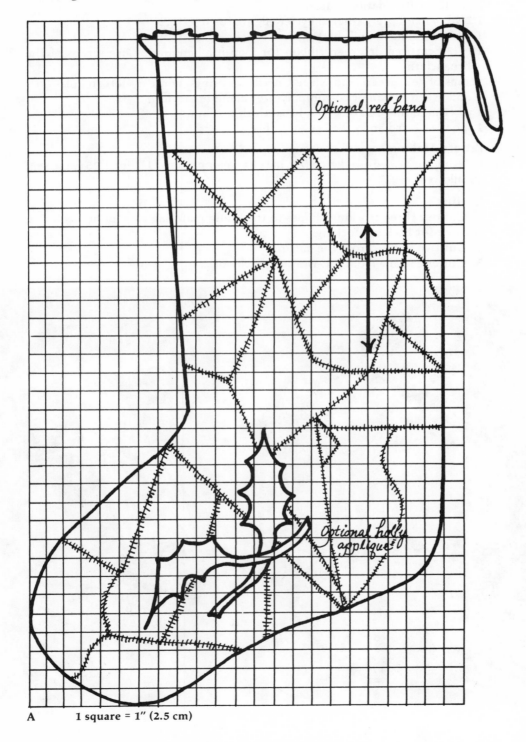

Optional red band

Optional holly applique

A   **1 square = 1" (2.5 cm)**

3. Sew down the patches using a machine decorative stitch or plain machine satin stitch. Continue working from side to side until the stocking shape is covered, except for 5" (12.5 cm) at the top of the stocking shape.

4. Cover this with a band cut 6" (15 cm) wide, with 1/2" (1.25 cm) turned under.

5. Repeat for the second side of the stocking (optional).

6. If you have a space that you cannot quite cover, machine applique in place a spray of holly leaves or bells.

Finishing

1. Make a "textile sandwich" with the back of stocking, batting, and lining.
2. Pin securely all around the leg and foot.
3. Cut off 1/2" (1.25 cm) from the top of the batting stocking shape.
4. Baste across the top to hold securely in place.
5. Stitch 1/8" (0.3 cm) from other edges to hold. *Do not omit this step as it makes all the rest of the assembly neater and faster.*
6. Assemble the front of the stocking in the same manner: crazy patchwork, batting, and lining.
7. Machine stitch together, using a generous 1/4" (0.6 cm) seam allowance, leaving the top of the stocking open.
8. Trim seams and clip to preserve the curve.
9. Turn right side out and *press very lightly around the edges only.*
10. Add the eyelet trim so that it stands up all around the top. If desired, the top of the stocking can be finished with straight or bias binding.
11. Add a loop for hanging the stocking by cutting a strip 2" (5 cm) by 12" (30 cm).
12. Press in 1/4" (0.6 cm) on each long edge.
13. Fold in half and stitch along edges to secure the loop.

Crazy Patchwork Christmas Tree Ornaments

These machine pieced and machine embroidered ornaments use a variety of Christmas red, green, and white print materials to create a country Victorian look for your Christmas decorations.

Technique Used   Modern materials machine method

Techniques Suitable   All

Materials Required

1 yd (1 m) 42" (105 cm) wide foundation material
1-1/2 yds (1.5 m) red, white, and green Christmas prints, plain red, plain green broadcloth, and white eyelet
1 yd (1 m) bonded quilt batting
1/4 yd (22.5 cm) white eyelet
1 yd (1 m) red or green plain broadcloth for backing of ornaments
1 spool each red and green machine embroidery thread

Pattern Making

1. Using the patterns given on page 130 (A), draw out each ornament onto cardboard for templates and set aside.

Laying Out

1. Assemble the backing, batting, and pin together with batting on top.
2. Refer to page 16 for modern machine method patchwork.
3. Make up the entire yard into crazy patchwork; keep the patches no bigger than 3" (7.5 cm) all around so that the scale is good for the smaller items.

Embellishment

1. Using the embroidery stitches on your machine, cover the seams with red or green (or both) stitching.

Cutting

1. Cut out the shape of the ornament.
2. Cut out the backing for each ornament. For maximum speed, pin the broadcloth to the underside of the worked top and cut as one unit. Be sure your scissors are sharp!

Making Up

1. With right sides together, sew the lining to the worked top of each ornament.
2. Clip any curved seams, turn, and press.
3. Stuff with quilt batting — not too tightly.

Finishing

1. Ornaments can be individualized with lace, ribbons, or other types of trim.
2. Add a crocheted or ribbon loop for hanging.

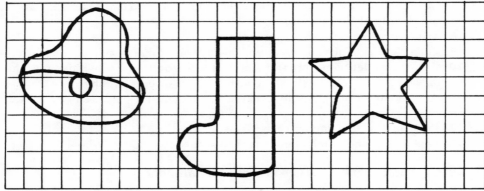

A   **1 square = 1" (2.5 cm)**   *Add 1/4" (0.6 cm) seam allowance*

Crazy Patchwork Shadow Quilted Christmas Hanging

Crazy patchwork can often be combined with other needlework and quilting techniques to create interesting and original works. Louise Rask of Copper Cliff, Ontario, one of my students, created this hanging using the techniques of shadow quilting and crazy patchwork.

Techniques Used   Shadow quilting and modern materials method

Techniques Suitable   Same

Materials Required

1 yd (1 m) olive green cotton or cotton/polyester blend broadcloth, 45" (112.5 cm) wide

1 fabric gluestick

1/2 yd (45 cm) bonded polyester quilt batting

1/2 yd (45 cm) polyester sheer dotted swiss (Look in drapery departments for this material.)

Scraps of polyester double knit or felt in Christmas red, dark green, white, yellow, and one small piece of brown

1/4 yd (22.5 cm) narrow ribbon in each color — white, red, and yellow

Scrap of red ribbon, 1/4" (0.6 cm) wide and 12" (30 cm) long

Two small jingle bells

White quilting thread

Olive green sewing thread

Red ribbon, 1" (2.5 cm) wide and 15" (37.5 cm) long for hangers

Small brass rod 18" (45 cm) long with knobs on the end

Pattern Making

1. Using the sketch given (A), enlarge the design.
2. Cut out the pattern shapes for the bells, packages, Christmas tree, tub, star, and moon. *Note: Seams are allowed in the patterns and measurements.*

Cutting

1. Cut two rectangles of green 16" (40 cm) wide and 24" (60 cm) long.
2. Cut a rectangle of batting the same dimensions.
3. Cut a rectangle of dotted swiss, also the same dimensions.
4. Cut two red bells from polyester knit (or you can substitute felt).
5. Cut one square package and one rectangular package from red polyknit.
6. Cut one square and one rectangular package from white polyknit.
7. Cut one square and one rectangular package from yellow polyknit.
8. Cut one red tub from red polyknit.
9. Cut one dark brown tree trunk from felt or polyknit.
10. Cut one yellow star and one white half-moon from polyknit or felt.

Laying Out

1. Fold one green rectangle in four to find the centre.
2. Lay out the tree pattern with bottom of tree 10" (25 cm) from the bottom and about 7" (17.5 cm) from the top. Position by eye for effect.
3. With a pencil, lightly trace around the pattern.
4. Lay out scraps of red, white, dark green, and yellow polyknit within that shape; pin in place.
5. Top with the yellow star; pin in place.
6. Position the two bells in the upper left corner about 5" (12.5 cm) from the top and 2" (5 cm) from the side; pin in place.
7. Position tree trunk and tub and pin.
8. Position the moon in the upper right corner.

9. Position the packages in the lower left and right corners and pin.

10. Put the trim in place on the packages and pin.

11. When design is satisfactory, fasten each of the elements in place with fabric glue.

Making Up

1. Place one layer of olive green broadcloth on the table.

2. Place the bonded quilt batt on top.

3. Next place the design layer of the hanging in place.

4. Cover with the dotted swiss material.

5. Pin or baste carefully. If pinning, use small gold safety pins and pin from the centre out.

6. With the white quilting thread and using a small quilting stitch, outline the bells, the tree, the star, the moon, and the packages.

Embellishment

1. The hanging shown is not embellished with stitches, but if you want to work the embroidery stitches over the patches, work them at this stage and through the dotted swiss and first layer of green only.

Finishing

1. Bring the edges of the hanging from the back to the front and turn under the raw edges, mitring the corners as shown on pages 51-53.

2. Hand stitch in place using a slipstitch or decorate if you like with line embroidery stitches.

3. Sew the jingle bells in place (A).

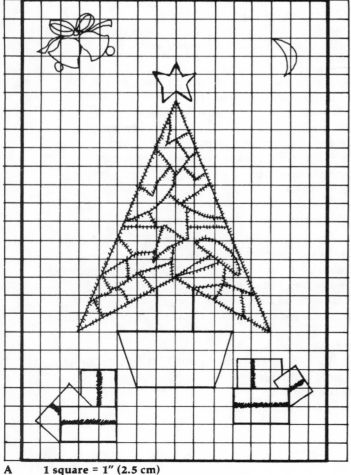

A   1 square = 1" (2.5 cm)

4. Tie a red bow, notching the ends of the ribbon, and tack in place over the tops of the bells on the *outside* of the dotted swiss.

5. Cut the wider red ribbon into four lengths of 3″ (7.5 cm) each and notch both ends.

6. Fold in half and machine stitch the notched ends in place for hangers.

7. Hang from a brass cafe curtain rod.

HANDBAGS, TOTE BAGS, GLASSES CASE
San Diego Spring Handbag

I had enough material left over from making the San Diego Spring jacket to make a handbag. I used one of my favorite handbag patterns for this. The bag has a flap which effectively keeps things from falling out. It is roomy and sturdy but very quickly made.

Technique Used   Semi-traditional with variation I

Techniques Suitable   All

Materials Required
3/4 yd (67.5 cm) coral lining material, 45″ (112.5 cm) wide
3/4 yd (67.5 cm) bonded quilt batting, 45″ (112.5 cm) wide
Scraps of print in aqua, rust, terra cotta, coral, brown, and sage green as used in the jacket
Scraps of coral and rosewood and sage green Ultrasuede™
1 ball each sage green and rosewood #8 pearl cotton
1/2 yd (45 cm) terra cotta lining material for bias binding
Rust and aqua sewing thread
1 wooden toggle or large button

Left: Tote bag; middle: summer and winter handbags; right: San Diego Spring handbag.

Pattern Making

1. This handbag requires no drafted pattern.

Cutting

1. Cut two rectangles of lining 15" (37.5 cm) x 13" (32.5 cm).
2. Cut two pieces the same size from batting.
3. Cut one strip of backing and one of batting 36" x 4" (90 cm x 10 cm) for the boxing band (B).
4. Trace off the pattern piece for the flap (given full-size) (A).
5. Cut one flap in batting, one in backing, and one in aqua.
6. Cut and make up bias binding as directed on page 57.
7. Cut two handle strips 22" x 3" (55 cm x 7.5 cm) in rust, two in aqua, and two in batting.

Laying Out

1. Lay one bag side lining, face down, on table and cover with one bonded batt shape.
2. Starting at the upper left corner, cover with scraps using the semi-traditional method with variation I as discussed on page 17.
3. Repeat for other side.
4. Lay boxing band lining, face down, on the table and cover with the piece of batting.
5. Cover with scraps in the semi-traditional method with variation I.

Embellishment

1. Use the same stitches as used for the jacket.
2. Use some of the same stitch combinations as on the jacket, scaling them down a little.
3. Use some embroidered and appliqued motifs in Ultrasuede™ and material as described in the directions for the jacket.

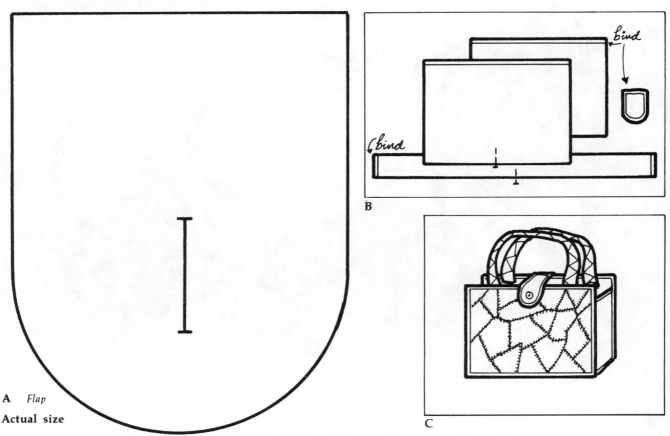

A   *Flap*

Actual size

B

C

Making Up

1. With the bias binding, (see bias binding application on page 59), finish the top edges of the bag and the short ends of the boxing strip, as well as going completely around the flap (B).
2. Find the centre point of the boxing strip and mark with a pin.
3. Find the centre point of the two sides and mark with pins.
4. Match and with *wrong* sides together pin the band around the bag. *Raw edges will be out.*
5. Sew in place by machine.
6. Using the bias stripping, and starting at one corner, completely cover the seams on each side. Hand or machine finish.
7. Sandwich aqua, rust, and batting handle strips and machine around three sides; turn and stitch closed. I also machine quilted the handles for extra strength and firmness.

Finishing

1. Machine stitch flat buttonhole or work by hand.
2. Machine stitch the other (straight) edge of the flap to one side of the bag.
3. Mark place for toggle and put on.
4. Attach handles by machine for strength in position (C).

Crazy Patchwork Handbag (Two Variations)

This versatile crazy patchwork bag can be as casual or as elegant as you care to make it. The size, fabric selected, threads chosen for the decorative stitching, and the scale of the patchwork all contribute to the effect you want and the use to which it will be put. If the bag is made up in jewel tones of amethyst and turquoise with rich violet pearl cotton embroidery, it is a perfect autumn handbag.

The second variation is made up somewhat smaller in scale in pastel prints of yellow, rose, mint green, orange ice, pale turquoise, blue, and mauve teamed with white eyelet and stitched and lined in sunny yellow.

It is not necessary to crazy patchwork both sides of the bag; a decorated front will provide ample embellishment.

Technique Used   Semi-traditional with variation I

Technique Suitable   Same

Materials Required

1/2 yd (45 cm) foundation fabric (This can be well-washed sheeting or any lightweight, preshrunk material, even medium-weight interfacing material.)

Brown paper or tissue paper for pattern

1/2 yd (45 cm) of thick quilt batting, preferably bonded, for body and sturdiness

Sewing thread in a color that blends with all your scraps

1 ball #8 pearl embroidery cotton

1/2 yd (45 cm) plain material or prequilted cotton for lining (I used navy with tiny polka dots for the winter bag and yellow for the summer bag. Use prequilted fabric for lining if you want an especially sturdy bag.)

1 pair of D-shaped purse handles

1 yd (1 m) polyester fold-over braid (I used navy for the winter bag and yellow for the summer bag.)

Scraps of cotton or cotton/polyester blend in the color scheme of your choice

Hints for making attractive crazy patchwork for the bags
Use at least five different materials although you may choose a monochromatic color scheme if you wish. Unless you plan to launder the bag, washability is not a factor in choosing the scraps. You may have to "creatively" trim some of your scraps to a more suitable size or shape, keeping them scaled to the size of your project — small ones for an evening bag, medium ones for a handbag, and larger ones for a tote bag. Good balance is achieved in your design if you can arrange to use each color family at least three times. I find it helpful to sort the scraps into colors, set them up in a pleasing order, and use the scraps in that order as I sew.

Pattern Making

1. Check the section on making patterns and enlarge the sketch given here (A) to the size you wish.

Everyday Size

1. Cut a piece of brown paper or tissue paper 17" (42.5 cm) long and 15-1/2" (38.75 cm) wide.
2. Fold in half so it is 17" (42.5 cm) long and 7-1/4" (18.2 cm) wide.
3. Measure up 12" (30 cm) and mark point X.
4. From the fold line to the open edge of the paper measure 5" (12.5 cm), mark point Y; and from the bottom edge up 5" (12.5 cm), mark point Z.
5. Freehand style, connect point Y to X.
6. Continue to draw a gently curved line from X to Z.
7. Cut out and open for the pattern piece for bag and lining; it includes 5/8" (1.5 cm) seam allowance.

To Reduce the Size

1. Cut a second pattern from brown paper.
2. Freehand, cut the pattern down until the size and shape satisfies you. Remember that the seam allowance is included; you may have to make several patterns until the size is suitable.

Using the Grid

1. The pattern is given here on a grid if you prefer to use this method of pattern drafting. The size shown is 1" (2.5 cm) per square. If you want a smaller bag, use 1/2" (1.25 cm) per square.

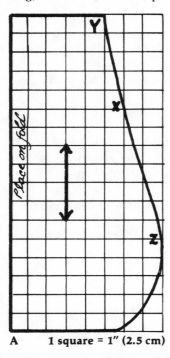

A   1 square = 1" (2.5 cm)

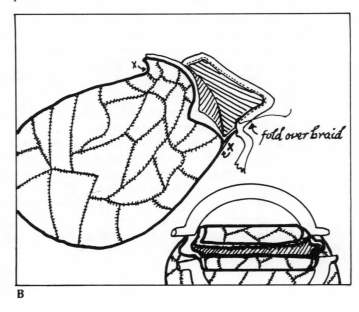

fold over braid

B

Cutting (outer shell of purse)

1. Cut out two shapes in the foundation fabric and two in the batting.
2. *Do not cut out the lining* until you have worked the front of the bag; the crazy patchwork and the embroidery will "take up" considerable material.

Laying Out

1. Machine baste the batting to the foundation. (If your machine foot catches in the batting, wrap a piece of cellophane tape over the toe of the foot.)
2. Lay out your selection of fabrics and determine an order in which you will sew them.

Sewing

1. Follow directions for semi-traditional patchwork with variation I.
2. If there are some small raw edges or spots left in the body of the purse, cover these with applique shapes such as circles, hearts, or flower shapes. This helps to relieve the rather angular lines of the machine-sewn patches. Note the heart-shaped applique on the yellow bag and the circle on the winter bag.
3. Trim any overhanging edge to conform with the shape of the bag. You may baste (hand or machine) around the outside edge to keep shapes in order.

Embellishment

Summer Bag   Every seam is covered with embroidery. Stitches used include cross-stitch (around the heart); outline stitch (for "Mary"); open cretan stitch; open cretan stitch with detached chain; detached chain; zigzag chain; single, double, and triple featherstitch; blanket stitch; herringbone stitch; detached fly stitch with straight flat stitch.

Winter Bag   Not every seam is stitched over with embroidery stitches. Put embellishment on only about one-third of the seamlines, being sure to distribute the stitching evenly over the surface of the bag. Try this and if you do not like the rather contemporary effect it creates, fill in the rest of the seamlines for a more traditional look. The stitches used are open cretan stitch; herringbone; single, double, and triple featherstitch; zigzag chain; detached fly stitch; open and closed blanket stitch.

Making Up

1. Cut out the lining pieces using the worked parts as your pattern.
2. If you want a key/change pocket in your bag, attach it before assembling the lining. Cut two pieces of lining material 4" by 3" (10 cm by 7.5 cm). Sew around three sides, insert a piece of batting the same size and sew it closed. Quilt the piece, then machine sew it to the lining around three sides.
3. Machine stitch the lining pieces from X to X (B), right sides together.
4. Machine sew the front and back of the outer shell together, right sides together, from X to X. Turn to right side and press if necessary.
5. Insert lining into outer shell and pin both layers together. Check to be sure that the opening is sufficiently large to get in and out of when using the bag. If not, enlarge the opening by ripping open the seam a little more (equally) on each side.
6. Machine sew the fold-over braid over the raw edges, starting at one seamline and working continuously around to the seamline, overlapping the raw edge and turning under the raw edge of the braid (B).
7. Insert the top ends of the bag into the handles through the slots.
8. Handsew the braid to the lining using a double length of color-coordinating quilting or embroidery thread (for strength). Be sure not to stitch through to the front.

Go-Anywhere Clutch-Style Bag

This useful bag is so easily made you'll want to have several to go with different outfits. It is equally appropriate for an elegant evening or an afternoon. The choice of fabrics makes the difference. The bag pictured is for evenings, designed and made by Doreen Campbell in a workshop on crazy patchwork. The black velvets used are a perfect foil for the sparkling silver lamé and the purple and violet silks, satins, and brocades. If you like to have your hands free, a length of chain makes a chic strap.

Technique Used   Traditional

Techniques Suitable   All

Materials Required

1/4 yd (22.5 cm) of sturdy muslin, cotton gabardine, or lightweight denim to use as the foundation and give body to the purse when finished

1/4 yd (22.5 cm) heavyweight, bonded polyester quilt batting, doubled (This is also necessary to give stability to the purse.)

1/4 yd (22.5 cm) black silk lining material

Scraps of black velvet, silver lamé, and different purple and violet silks, satins, and brocades

1 ball bright violet #8 pearl cotton or various silk threads

2 velcro dots in matching color *or* 2 large fabric-covered snaps

Pattern Making

This bag is so simple you don't even have to make a paper pattern.

1. On your foundation material measure out and mark a rectangle 22" (55 cm) long and 12" (30 cm) wide. Be sure to keep your grain lines straight (a carpenter's or dressmaker's T-square is great for this (A).

2. Cut a double layer of batting the same size.

3. Cut a rectangle of the black silk lining also the same size.

Laying Out

1. If you use any of the three semi-traditional methods, put the batting on top of the foundation material and proceed to lay out your scraps in a pleasing design.

Pinning and Basting

1. Pin and/or baste the pieces in place as required by the technique you chose.

2. Overlap and underlap pieces as necessary.

Embellishment

1. Suggested stitches are double and triple featherstitch; chain-based variations; herringbone-based variations; blanket stitch variations; and lots of textural interest with such stitches as french knot; bullion knot; coral stitch; and palestrina knot.
2. Press, face down, on a turkish towel when stitching is complete.

Note: This is the place to use your fanciest stitches and most elaborate stitch combinations.

Making Up

1. If you want an even sturdier bag, add another layer of quilt batting.
2. Make a "textile sandwich" with quilt batting on the bottom, the embellished top *right side up* and the lining material on top, *right side down*.
3. Machine stitch around all four sides leaving a 5" (12.5 cm) opening for turning (A).
4. Trim seams and notch corners.
5. Turn carefully, pulling out the corners well.
6. Press, face down, on a turkish towel. Be sure that none of the lining shows on the right side.

Finishing

1. With matching thread and fine, close whipstitches, turn in the raw edges and close the opening.
2. Fold in three (B).
3. Mark with pins where the folds fall.
4. Turn to the inside and with matching thread, *doubled for strength,* sew the lower bag sides closed. Use fine, close whipstitches and begin and finish securely.
5. Turn back to the right side (outside of bag).
6. If you want a brass or silver chain, check your hardware store or look in a costume jewelery department for an attractive one to use as a shoulder or hand strap. Shoulder straps will need to be 24" (60 cm) long and hand straps should be 12" (30 cm) long. Hand sew the lower edges of the chains into place. Be sure not to go through to the front side.
7. Using velcro dots that match in color or fabric-covered large snaps, hand sew them on the inner flap and outer top edge of the bag (C). Be careful *not to* sew through to the front outside of the bag.

Note: Daytime bags look smashing in colorful corduroy, polyester and wool knits, or wool materials. Ultrasuede™ or the real thing add a touch of luxury.

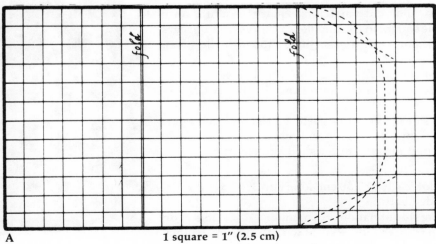

A

1 square = 1" (2.5 cm)
The front flap can be cut in any shape

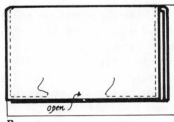

B

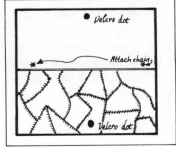

C

Square Tote with Crazy Patchwork Panel

This generously sized tote bag is very easy to make and has exceptionally sturdy construction. Use it for toting your library books, quilting projects, knitting, and other miscellanea we all carry around.

Technique Used   Semi-traditional

Techniques Suitable   All

Materials Required

12" (30 cm) square of soft foundation fabric

1 yd (1 m) cotton print for the outside in turquoise floral

1 yd (1 m) cotton for the lining in navy blue pin dot

1 yd (1 m) *bonded* batting (double this for a heavier bag)

Scraps of material in the color scheme of your choice, at least five different materials (Colors might include plain purple, purple floral, purple pin dot, turquoise floral, turquoise pin dot, and grey floral.)

Pattern Making

No pattern is required for this bag.

Laying Out

1. Fold the 12" (30 cm) square in half diagonally and in half again and press.
2. Applique in place an 8" (20 cm) square of purple and proceed to quilt it.
3. An alternative approach is to applique in place a 4" (10 cm) square.
4. Lay out the crazy pieces until you are satisfied with the arrangement.
5. Proceed to sew them with the semi-traditional technique (see page 16).

Embellishment

All or only some of the seamlines may be embellished. The stitches used on the bag in the photograph are open cretan; herringbone; attached fly stitch; single, double, and triple featherstitch; blanket stitch variations I and II; zigzag chain. Combinations and other variations may be used according to your imagination and inclination. I used C V, C XI in a daisy motif. Measure and trim the panel if it has been pulled out of shape while working on it.

Making Up

1. Cut two strips of turquoise floral, each 12" (30 cm) long and 3" (7.5 cm) wide. Sew these to the top and bottom of the embellished panel.
2. Cut two strips 18" (45 cm) long and 3" (7.5 cm) wide and sew to the two opposite sides.
3. Press.
4. Using the completed front as a guide, cut a matching square from turquoise floral *or* using an 8" (20 cm) purple square in the middle, add successive borders of turquoise floral and navy pin dot, each measuring 2" (5 cm) wide when finished. Press.
5. Seam together the bottoms of the outer shell of the tote. Press.
6. Using this as a guide, cut a rectangle for the lining and another two layers from bonded batting.
7. Pin the batting to the wrong side of the outer shell and seam up the sides.
8. Seam the sides of the lining, right sides together. Press.
9. Insert the lining, wrong side out, into the outer shell and pin in place.

Finishing

1. Cut two handles of navy pin dot, each 20" (50 cm) long and 3" (7.5 cm) wide. Cut two matching strips of bonded batting.
2. Place bonded batting on wrong side of handle, turn under 1/2" (1.25 cm) on each long side and machine stitch from the top. Repeat with the second handle.

3. Pin handles in place turning under 1/2" (1.25 cm) all around at top of bag, being sure that the raw edges of the handle are tucked between the outer shell and the lining piece.

4. Top stitch all around by machine, catching both handles as you go.

Crazy Patchwork Glasses Case

A smart glasses case is a necessary accessory for a modern woman. Whether used for designer sunglasses, reading glasses, or simply for an extra pair of "specs" this quickly-made case makes a glamorous and very welcome gift. It is a generous size and easily accommodates fashionable over-size glasses.

Technique Used   Traditional

Techniques Suitable   All

Materials Required

1/8 yd (11.25 cm) or a piece of prequilted silk coat lining in any color that is 18" (45 cm) long and 5" (12.5 cm) wide

Scraps of silk or scraps of cottons and cotton blends (Since this is an accessory that is handled a great deal, choose dark colors that do not show the soil.) Ribbon looks smart on this case

1-1/2 yds (1.5 m) dark-colored grosgrain ribbon, 1-1/2" (3.75 cm) wide

Gold-colored #8 pearl cotton

Sewing thread to match the color of the prequilted lining

1 velcro dot closure to harmonize in color with the lining and the patchwork

Pattern Making

1. See the accompanying sketch for the pattern (A).

Cutting

1. Cut the material 17" (42.5 cm) long and 5" (12.5 cm) wide.
2. Mark off the flap on the pattern and trim one end to shape.

Laying Out

1. On the *wrong* side of the quilted material pin the scraps in a pleasing order. (See traditional technique, page 16.)
2. Baste down, underlapping and overlapping as necessary.

Embellishment

1. Embroider along the seamlines. *Be careful not to take the thread through to the quilted side.*
2. Suggested stitches include herringbone; single, double, and triple feather-stitch; petal stitch; open cretan; open and closed buttonhole stitch; cable chain; zigzag chain; detached and attached fly stitch.
3. Combination stitches can be used and decorative motifs can be used that have some personal meaning for the person who will use the glasses case.

Making Up

1. Using the grosgrain ribbon, machine sew as a binding over the short, straight end.
2. Fold the case as shown (B) and starting at the lower left corner, use the ribbon to bind the raw edges of the case, taking it up and around the flap and down the right side to the bottom.
3. Be sure to turn under the raw ends of the ribbon neatly and hand sew in place with a very fine, close whipstitch in the color of the ribbon.
4. Add a velcro dot closure to the inner flap and the centre top of the case.

Note: This case can be made up using scraps of material for lining, bonded quilt batting scraps large enough to cut out the shape, and the semi-traditional method with variation I. The binding can be done by making your own straight-edge or bias binding as shown on pages 55, 57.

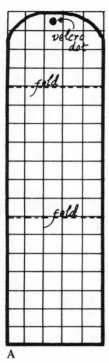

A

1 square = 1" (2.5 cm)

B

C

HOUSEHOLD ITEMS

Pillows, Pillows, Pillows

One of the best ways to perk up a room is by adding colorful patchwork pillows cleverly designed to pull together the color scheme or add that necessary special accent to a neutral decor. The materials used and the method of finishing the pillow determines its character. A pale blue antique satin paired with a chintz in pale blue and lemon yellow or a lemon yellow slubbed satin with a crisp piped finish can pick up the floral chintz of the drapes. A dark brown and white gingham and country-style print with a deep wide brown ruffle sings out "country" and all the comfy, cozy warmth that goes with the style. A sophisticated color scheme of avocado green, burgundy, and rose is entirely different in character and may be one you'd choose for your home or apartment. Here is a selection of pillows to inspire you.

Technique Used   Traditional

Techniques Suitable   All

General instructions will be given here for the construction of the pillows shown in the photograph.

Size

Pillows may be made in any size, but for general purposes of decoration the 18" (45 cm) square pillow is best.

Pillow Top

1. This is constructed as described in the technique chosen, on a foundation cut to size.

Filling

1. You can buy pillow forms (in which case buy the form first and tailor the top to the form available) or you can stuff your own, usually with polyester stuffing (not quilt batt).
2. If you want a rather flat pillow you can use several layers of comforter batting basted together to keep them from separating.

Edge Finishes

Plain seam   This is the easiest to do. Place right sides of the top and bottom together and seam around by machine with a generous 5/8" (1.5 cm) seam allowance. Leave a 6" (15 cm) opening in the centre of one side for turning; pull out the corners well and press the seams.

Cording   This is a little harder but the crisp, tailored effect it gives is worth the effort and it also strengthens the edge of the pillow helping it to wear longer! In any notions department find some cable cord in the correct diameter for your project; remember scale is important in design. Cut the fabric strips for covering the cord on the bias so that the cord will go around corners easily. If you want to use straight strips to cover the cord, clip the seam allowance frequently to make up for the lack of "give" (it is this "give" that makes bias binding so great). Proceed with the following steps.

1. To get the width of the fabric strip that covers the cord, measure the circumference of the cord by wrapping a tape measure around it (not too tightly) and add 1" to 1-1/4" (2.5 cm to 3.2 cm) to it.
2. To get the length of strip needed, measure the outer edge of the pillow top and add 4" (10 cm).
3. Cover the cord by folding your cloth strip (right side out) in half, around the cable cord (A). Be sure the cording is nearest the fold.
4. Use a zipper foot to sew close to the cording.

5. Stitch the cording onto the pillow top (B). Leave about 2" (5 cm) on the end on which you start the stitching. Start at the centre of any of the sides.

6. Pin the cording in place so that the stitching line on the cording lies exactly on the seam of the pillow top.

7. Use the zipper foot again to sew it on, using your hand stitching on the cording as a guide.

8. To turn the corner, stitch up to the corner, leave the needle in the fabric, and clip the fabric three or four times in the seam allowance where it will go around the corner (B). The cording will spread out as it goes around the corner and it will lie smoothly, so pivot with the needle still in the fabric and continue to sew.

9. As you come to the beginning, leave about 2" (5 cm) for joining (C).

10. Join the two ends by unpicking the stitching and opening up the bias on one end. Cut away enough cord so that the two ends of the cord meet exactly.

11. Turn under about 1/4" (0.6 cm) on the cut-off end and lap over the beginning end.

12. Stitch through all the thicknesses of the fabric.

13. Finish in the same way for all pillows.

Ruffles   Ruffles add a feminine, informal look to pillows. Ruffles may be a single layer of fabric with a narrow hem (if you use your narrow hemmer on the sewing machine, it's a fantastic timesaver!), or a double thickness of fabric with the raw edges hidden in the seam. I prefer a double ruffle. For all ruffles, however, the technique is the same.

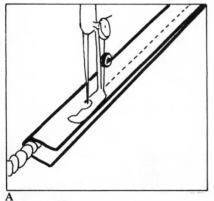
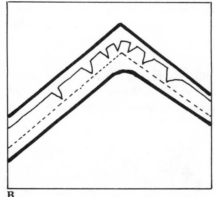
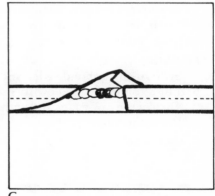

A   B   C

t: Pillow designed by Susan Gore of Sudbury, Ontario.
ght: Necktie pillow designed by Margaret Osen of Roberts, Wisconsin.

Pillow designed by Carol Smith of Toronto, Ontario.

1. To get the size, measure around the outside of the pillow. For a *very* full, luxurious ruffle, measure it two and one-half times the length and double the width. For a less expensive ruffle, one and one-half to two times the length will work with the double width.

2. There are several ways to gather a ruffle.

By hand   This is tedious but neat. Use a double thread in your needle so it does not break at a crucial point and take medium-sized running stitches. Do each side separately; otherwise, it is hard to adjust the ruffles.

By machine   A "ruffler-pleater" is an inexpensive attachment to your machine that will be a joy. It works like a charm turning out yards of ruffles in literally minutes. It can be adjusted for full or less full ruffles.

Without a machine attachment the best way to ruffle is to use your zigzag foot and a length of pearl cotton (or string in a pinch) the length of the unruffled strip. Pin the string in place where you want the ruffling to take place and using a *large* zigzag stitch, one that *covers it but does not catch it*, stitch the length of the cord. Then pull up and adjust to fit.

3. Seam the ends of the strip together by machine. I like to use a french or double seam; I sew a narrow seam, wrong sides together and then a larger seam, right sides together, completely enclosing the raw edges.

4. Adjust the ruffles to fit the perimeter of the pillow (D).

5. Pin the ruffle in place on the front of the pillow, raw edges of ruffle to raw edges of pillow top.

6. Machine baste in place.

7. See directions below for making the back of pillows. Then with the back of the pillow in place, right side down, machine sew the three layers together, leaving a 6" (15 cm) opening for turning.

Finishing

1. Stuff, using unbonded doll and pillow stuffing or handfulls of *unbonded* quilt batt or a commercial pillow form. Be sure the corners are well-filled.

2. Turn in the raw edges and with a fine, close whipstitch in a matching thread, close the opening.

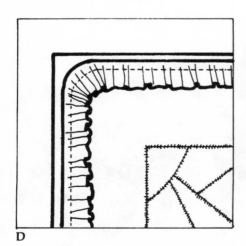

Detail of ruffled pillow on page 143.

Pillow Back (Envelope Closure)

If you want to be able to remove the pillow casing for laundering or dry cleaning, it is best to make an envelope closure.

Pattern Making

1. Measure the width of the pillow form and add 1/2" (1.25 cm) seam allowance on each side plus a 1" (2.5 cm) hem allowance.
2. Divide the resulting figure in half and cut one paper pattern this wide by the length of the pillow plus 1/2" seam allowance on each side.

Cutting

1. Cut two pieces from this pattern.

Making Up

1. Hem the edges of the overlap and underlap 1/4" (0.6 cm) and then 1/4" (0.6 cm) again.
2. Overlap and underlap these pieces 3" (7.5 cm) as shown (E), and pin. Your pillow back should now be the same size as your pillow front.

Sewing

1. Pin the pillow front and back together, right sides facing.
2. Machine sew all around, pivoting at the corners and finishing off securely.
3. Trim seams and notch corners.

Finishing

1. Turn the front through to the right through the envelope opening, press, and insert pillow form.

Note: In the photograph on page 143, the pillow that shows a selection of neckties (twelve or more), taken apart and drycleaned (or washed if washable) makes an exciting combination of textures and colors. This pillow is now a conversation-piece in Margaret Osen's home. There are many more ways to make pillows, using any of the crazy patchwork techniques. I highly recommend a book by Mary Elizabeth Johnson, Pillows, *Oxmoor House, Birmingham, Alabama, 1978. This is available either from your public library or if you want to own it write to The Book Division, Progressive Farmer Company, P.O. Box 2463, Birmingham, Alabama, 35202.*

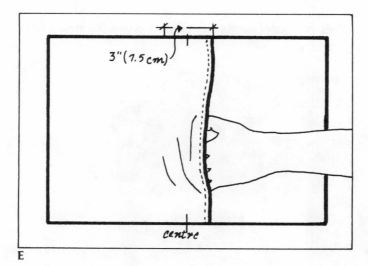

3" (7.5 cm)

centre

E

A Box for Dreams

Everyone needs a very special treasure chest. It should be fittingly lovely to store the precious moments of our lives — some old love letters, the envelope with a tiny wisp of baby's first curls, a card signed in your mother's hand-writing from the very last gift she ever gave you. We all have our treasured mementos. This black moiré taffeta box with satin, velvet, silk, and brocade crazy patchwork spilling gracefully over the top of the box and along the front makes a fitting repository for these dreams. When made as a gift for someone it can hold a trifle or stand on its own.

Technique Used   Traditional

Techniques Suitable   All

Materials Required

Box

Matt board 1-1/4" (3.1 cm) thick size, 1 yd (1 m) x 3/4 yd (67.5 cm)
X-Acto blade knife (available from any hobby shop)
Steel-edged ruler
White tacky glue
Quilt batting (bonded) 24" x 24" (60 cm x 60 cm)

Fabric covering

3/4 yd (67.5 cm) black taffeta moiré (any sturdy, stiff plain fabric will do)
Scraps of taffeta, silk, velvet, brocade, tie silks, plush, etc. (The colors I used were turquoise, purple, black, and gold with hot pink.)
1 ball purple #8 pearl cotton embroidery thread
1 commercially made black "frog" (fastener)

Pattern Making

1. The pieces needed are drawn directly onto the matt board and onto the moiré tafetta (A).

Box

1. With a sharp pencil, a steel-edged ruler, and great accuracy transfer the cutting diagram to the matt board.
2. Cut out the pieces carefully with the X-Acto knife, using the steel ruler to make sure the cuts are absolutely straight.
3. Gently sandpaper the cut edge of each piece of matt board to remove little burrs.

4. Cut the quilt batting using the same cutting diagram but be sure to cut two of each pattern piece — one for the inside and one for the outside of the box.
5. Using white glue, carefully glue a piece of quilt batting in place on one side of each matt board piece.
6. When dry, glue a second piece on the other side of the matt board and allow to dry thoroughly, preferably overnight.

Fabric covering

1. Using tailor's chalk (well-sharpened) or a sharp white marking pencil, transfer the diagram (A) to the *wrong* side of the moiré tafetta. Be very careful to maintain the grain of the material.
2. Cut out accurately.
3. On the *right side* of pieces 1 and 2 lay out your crazy patchwork pieces starting at the cut edge of the fabric and continuing diagonally to the opposite side. Note the suggested layout of pieces in diagram (B).

Pinning and Basting

1. When your layout pleases you, pin the pieces in place.
2. Hand baste in place. Make sure that the heavier fabric pieces are overlapped by lighter-weight pieces.
3. Turn edges under and baste in place.

Note: Basting is important because pins inevitably fall out and your arrangement will be lost if you use pins only.

Embellishment

1. With purple #8 pearl cotton secure the edges of the patchwork, using a variety of embroidery stitches and stitch combinations.
2. Stitches used on this project are fern stitch; plain and zigzag chain; single, double, and triple featherstitch; herringbone stitch; wheatear stitch; star stitch; open cretan; and detached fly stitch.
3. Use a few star stitches in the centre of plain pieces and use more elaborate stitch combinations on plain patches.
4. Remove basting and press pieces, face down, on a turkish towel.

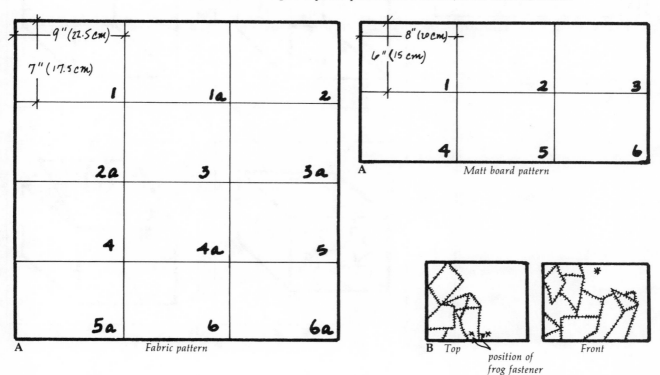

A   *Fabric pattern*

A   *Matt board pattern*

B   *Top*   *Front*

position of frog fastener

Making Up

1. With wrong sides of pieces 3 and 3a together, machine or hand sew around three sides using a 1/2" (1.25 cm) seam allowance.
2. Repeat with pieces 4 and 4a, 5 and 5a, 6 and 6a, 1 and 1a, 2 and 2a.
3. Gently turn each piece, being sure the corners are well poked out, and press.
4. Insert the matching cardboard foundation piece to check for fit. It should fit snugly. Adjust if necessary.
5. Remove cardboard, turn to wrong side again, trim seam allowances, and notch corners to reduce bulk (C).
6. Turn to right side and with a pin, gently pull out the corners and edges of the fabric envelope.
7. Press again if necessary.
8. Insert matching cardboard piece, turn the seam allowances in, and with a fine, neat whipstitch and matching black thread, close the envelope (D).

Finishing

1. Using matching black thread and either the ladder stitch or a fine, close whipstitch, sew sides 5 and 4 to the short ends of bottom piece 6 (E). Be sure to sew right up to the corners.
2. With the same stitch and piece 3 (the back of the box), sew in place (F).
3. Then sew the crazy patchwork front piece 2 in place (G).
4. Finally, add the lid piece 1 sewing only along the side adjoining the back piece 3 (H).
5. Sew the fasteners in place on the lid piece and on its matching position on the front of the box (see photograph of completed box on page 146).

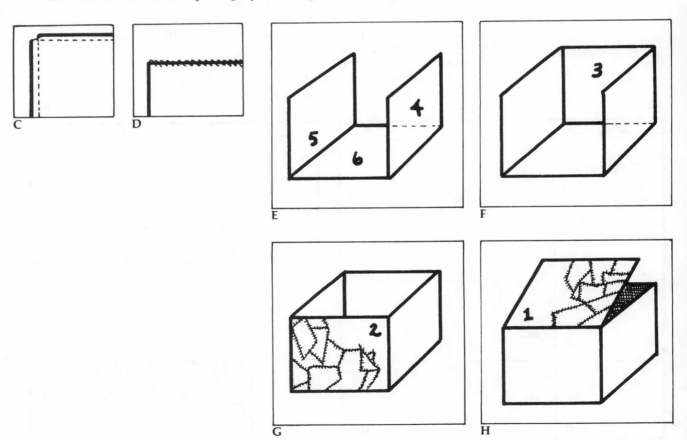

St. Clare of Assisi Wall Panel

St. Clare of Assisi was believed to have been the medieval patron saint of embroiderers. In 1966, the magazine of the English Embroiderers' Guild ran an article urging their members to celebrate the Diamond Jubilee of that organization by working a wall panel of a design to be made available to members (*Embroidery*, Summer, 1966, Vol. 17, No. 2). The interpretation of the design by six noted embroiderers was shown. With these photographs as inspiration I referred to some brass rubbings I own of similar design and adapted the given designs considerably. Unfortunately, there was no credit given to the original designer nor was any source for obtaining the pattern mentioned, and no author was noted for the article so I cannot give any credits. This project is my interpretation of that original idea; hopefully each of you will take the basic idea and feel free to interpret it in your own way, using crazy patchwork as your medium. St. Clare holds a monstrance, a container for the Blessed Sacrament. Tradition has it that she dispersed the Saracen invaders by facing them down with the monstrance in her hand to defend the convent she founded, the Order of Poor Clares. This fascinating information is found in Ulwood W. Post's *Saints, Signs and Symbols* (S.P.C.K., London, 1966).

Technique Used   Traditional

Materials Required

Background fabric of any evenly woven cloth in off-white or beige 54" x 26" (135 cm x 65 cm)

Scraps of rich fabrics in dark red, black, navy, royal blue, purple, olive, green, and gold

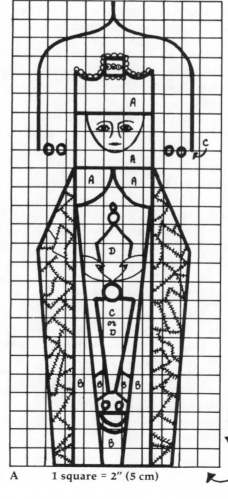

A   *Gold satin-appliqued*
B   *Royal blue satin*
C   *Gold braid*
D   *Blue and gold braid*

An additional 2" (5 cm) of fabric extends around this pattern for framing purposes

A   **1 square = 2" (5 cm)**

1/2 yd (45 cm) heavy gold-colored satin
1 yd (1 m) gold braid
Scraps of black and gold brocade for the monstrance
1 skein each gold and royal blue heavy rayon embroidery thread
1 large sequin
1 transfer pencil (available at notion departments or see mail order section)
1 ball gold-colored #8 pearl cotton
1 skein six-strand black embroidery thread
Stapler and staples (optional)

Pattern Making

1. Using the directions given in the pattern-making section, draft the pattern full-size, using tissue paper and the transfer pencil. Keep the pencil well sharpened as *lines will not wash out*. Please note the scale: 1 square equals 2" (5 cm). *Note: The pattern given is for size and suggested positioning. You will adapt the design to your own liking as shown in the photographed interpretation.*
2. Centre the pattern on your material and pin in place, face down.
3. With a hot iron transfer the pattern to the cloth. Be careful not to scorch your material.

Laying Out

1. Arrange your patches in a pleasing order, taking care to have the same number of patches of each color on each side of the cloak, but not in exactly the same place.
2. Pin and baste in place, underlapping and overlapping as necessary.

Embellishment

1. Embroider around each patch in gold-colored thread.
2. Stitches used in this piece are vandyke stitch (over the raw edges of velveteen patches which made a ridge when turned under); star stitch; single, double, and triple featherstitch; detached fly stitch; chain stitch; plain flat stitch; cross-stitch; blanket stitch in several variations; herringbone stitch; couching; and outline stitch. Combination stitches used were detached chain combination, chain, and star stitches.
4. There are no embroidered motifs on this work, apart from the spiral chain stitched royal blue roundels and the gold spider's webs.

Making Up

1. Using a fine black embroidery thread and using either outline stitch (as I did) or a small backstitch, stitch in the facial features and the hands.
2. Using your original pattern, cut out the shape of the monstrance and applique it in the black and gold brocade edged with gold braid.
3. Using the gold braid, outline the headdress and around the face.
4. Using the royal blue braid in several rows stitch the centre panel.
5. Stitch a gold roundel topped with mylar sequin at the top of the monstrance.
6. Trim the crown with gold braid (A).

Finishing

This is such a lovely piece you may wish to have it professionally framed. However, I used it for many years as described below before feeling I could afford to have it professionally framed.
1. Buy two stretcher bars (from an art supply or stationery store) each 50" (125 cm) long and two bars 22" (55 cm) long. This allows 4" (10 cm) for you to cover the depth of the stretcher bars.
2. Mark the centres of each side of the hanging and the centres of each side of the assembled frame.

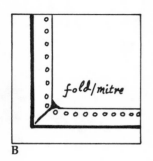

B

3. Lay the hanging right side down on a table, and place the frame right side down on it matching up the centre marks top and bottom.

4. Staple the top and bottom centre points first and then do the top, working from side to side to keep the tension even. You may use thumbtacks if a stapler is not available.

5. Repeat with the bottom.

6. Staple the centre point of each side and then working on one side only, staple alternately on each side of the point so the tension remains even.

7. Repeat for the other side.

8. Fold the corners in to mitre them and staple or tack in place (B).

9. Attach a picture hanger and hang in a place of honor.

Note: This design can be the basis of a series of church hangings or banners depicting various saints. Each saint should hold her/his own symbol. Good, clear, simple drawings of the symbols may be found in Ulwood W. Post's book, Saints, Signs and Symbols. *The same design base can be used for a series on women of the Bible as well. Some books you might find interesting are Dorothy Burchette's,* Needlework Blocking and Finishing, *1974 and* More Needlework Blocking and Finishing, *Charles Scribner Co., New York, 1979, and Katharine Ireys,* Finishing and Mounting Your Needlepoint Pieces, *Thomas Y. Crowell Company, New York, 1973.*

Victoriana Memorabilia

Adding richness and elegance to your decor or making a magnificant gift, this framed piece which incorporates mementos from pleasant events can act as a focal point and unify the color scheme of a room.

Technique Used   Traditional

Technique Suitable   Traditional

Materials Required

Select your frame first (new or antique)

Pictured is a new oval walnut frame 18" (45 cm) by 15" (37.5 cm), finished size (This frame can be hung vertically or horizontally and you should keep this in mind when planning to include small design motifs.)

A well-washed old sheet is perfect for the foundation material (This should be 3" (7.5 cm) larger all around than your finished size.)

Scraps of luxurious materials, about 3" (7.5 cm) across, in colors to harmonize with the decor (Include fragments of materials that hold precious memories as well. Remember to scale your patches to the size of the piece you are working — small piece, small-scale patches; large piece, large-scale patches.)
1 ball of gold colored #5 pearl embroidery cotton

Pattern Making
1. On the ironed foundation fabric lay the frame, face down, and trace the outline of the inner frame, using a color-fast ballpoint pen or pencil.

Laying Out
1. Unlike the placement of the patchwork in many of the other projects, this one is started in the centre and the patches laid outward from there.
2. Underlap heavy fabrics like velveteens to avoid a ridge.
3. Overlap the lighter-weight materials.

Pinning and Basting
1. When you are happy with the composition of your piece, baste it down, turning under the overlapped raw edges. Very heavy materials can be left and the raw edges covered by vandyke stitch.

Note: Leave the composition in a place where you can see it at odd moments for at least twenty-four hours so that you can rearrange the design. I use my dining room table which I pass frequently throughout the day.
2. Baste in place when completely satisfied.

Embellishment
Using a frame to work the stitches depends on your personal preference and the stitch being worked.
1. Stitches used on this piece are herringbone with variations; single, double, and triple featherstitch; attached and detached chain stitch; attached and detached fly stitch; open and closed cretan stitch; blanket stitch with variations; outline stitch; star stitch; backstitch; and vandyke stitch.

Note: This piece is an excellent vehicle for working small designs. I used a maple leaf, a unicorn, and a large star stitch on three of the larger plain patches. Best results for tiny motifs are obtained if a small backstitch is used for detail.

Making Up
1. The piece shown was done by a professional framer who stretched it beautifully.
2. If you choose to do it yourself, look up and follow the methods in Dorothy Burchette's excellent books or Katharine Irey's book (see References, page 151).

Crazy Patchwork Wedding Picture Frame

Soft fabric frames are easy to make, offer tremendous scope for creativity, and allow the maker to include mementos that will make the frames unique. Scraps of material from the dresses and trims from Sarah Jane's wedding are incorporated into this lovely frame which holds her wedding picture.

Technique Used   Traditional

Techniques Suitable   Semi-traditional with variations

Materials Required
For the frame
1 precut picture frame (see suppliers listed at end of project) *or*
Matt board 24" x 24" (60 cm x 60 cm) from framing or art supply shop
1/4 yd (22.5 cm) bonded quilt batting
Piece of worked crazy patchwork (in whatever technique you have chosen) 12"

(30 cm) square (If you use other frame sizes the important thing here is that the patchwork piece be 2" or 5 cm larger all around than the size of the frame you have chosen.)

Lightweight fusible interfacing, 12" (30 cm) square

White tacky crafter's glue that dries clear and is water soluble (Have a damp cloth handy for wiping gluey fingers!)

5 or 6 clamp-type clothespins and/or a heavy book

Craft knife or hobby knife with sharp blade (X-Acto knives are widely available.)

Fine sandpaper or emery board

Metal-edged ruler for guiding craft knife when cutting

Thick layer of old magazine, cardboard, or cutting board to protect your table when cutting the matt board

Note: If you are using a precut frame kit, go immediately to the instructions for padding and covering the frame.

Making Your Own Frame

1. Draft the pattern full-size onto paper.
2. Measure off your matt board (A).
3. Trace the frame shape once in each of the two 12" (30 cm) frame pieces.
4. Trace the centre opening piece onto one of them.
5. Trace off onto matt board the scaled-up easel stand pattern and the "spacer" patterns (make six of these).

Cutting

1. Using the craft knife, carefully and slowly cut out the oval opening for the centre of one frame piece. It usually takes several cuts in the same place to get a good sharp accurate cut. Angle the knife as necessary to preserve the curve.

2. Cut out the oval outside shapes of the two frame pieces.

3. Cut out the stand piece. Score the piece where shown in the diagram, so that the piece bends easily. *Do not cut all the way through.*

4. Cut out seven small spacer pieces from the left-over board. Keep any extra board pieces for use as spacer pieces in other frames.

5. With your fine sandpaper or emery board, smooth off edges.

Padding and Covering

1. Prepare your fabric by pressing it, face down, on a turkish towel.

2. Then apply the iron-on fusible interfacing to the wrong side of the material to stabilize it and prevent fraying. Follow the manufacturer's directions. Usually you need to use steam so be sure to use a press cloth to avoid water-spotting your materials.

3. Lay the front frame piece face down on the wrong side (fused) of the patchwork and trace around the oval opening with a sharp pencil (line 1) (B).

4. Using your ruler and a sharp pencil, draw another line 1/8" (0.3 cm) inside that (line 2) (B).

5. Draw in a third line 1/2" (1.25 cm) inside that again (line 3) (B).

6. Machine sew with a fine stitch on line 1, starting and stopping securely.

7. Using very sharp scissors, cut away the oval shape on the innermost (smallest) opening, line 3.

8. Clip from the cut edge to the second traced line about every 1/2" (1.25 cm). You may have to clip more closely later.

9. Set aside.

10. Cut two pieces of quilt batting exactly the same size as the front and back of the frame.

11. On one of these, trace the oval opening and carefully cut out with scissors.

12. Set aside.

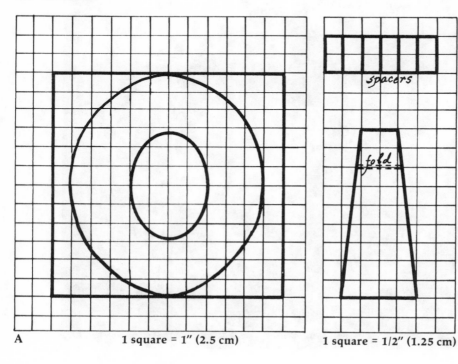

A   **1 square = 1" (2.5 cm)**   **1 square = 1/2" (1.25 cm)**

Putting on Fabric and Batting

1. Some trims can be put on at this stage.
2. Lay patchwork fabric, face down, on the working surface and carefully position the front frame on it.
3. Working with one small section at a time, starting in the centre of each side and cutting out small notches of material if necessary to preserve the curve, fold material back against the cardboard and glue (C).
4. Hold each small section in place until it sticks. Work alternately around the opening until all edges are glued.
5. Check front from time to time to be sure there are no wrinkles or clip marks. Be sure to clean your fingers frequently.
6. Set aside and let dry.

Inserting Batting

1. When the frame is dry, turn the board over and work from the right side.
2. Lift the unglued edges of the fabric and gently position the batting with the oval cut out on the board under the fabric.
3. Line up edges and opening evenly.
4. Smooth fabric down over batting.
5. Trim any excess batting so the batting is even with the outside edge of the frame.

Gluing Outside Edge of Front Frame

1. Work on one side at a time; the glue dries quickly.
2. Spread the glue along one edge of the back of the outer frame.
3. If there is excess material, cut tiny notches out of the outside edges (D).
4. Fold the fabric snugly to the back, check the front for wrinkles, and ease out.
5. When satisfied, clamp with clothespins. *Do not leave on longer than ten minutes or the clothespins will mark your frame.*
6. If you are using a frame with square corners, cut a small notch out of the corners to get rid of excess material and then fold.

Trims such as commercial silk cordings, homemade piping, small lace edging, ruffles, rickrack, ribbon (velvet, satin, grosgrain, etc), braid, or bias tape may be applied at this point. They may be sewn or glued on. Use only very small amounts of glue or it may ooze out and spoil the frame.

Covering the Back Frame Piece

1. Glue the batting in place on one side of piece and let dry.
2. Cover with material as described above and let dry.

Note: If your frame is designed to be given without a photo in it, cover the other side of the frame with fabric, but do not use any batting.

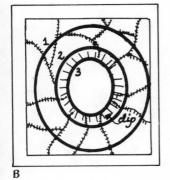

B

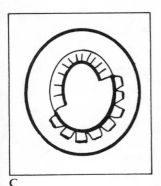

C

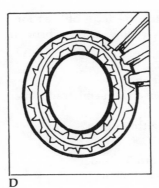

D

E

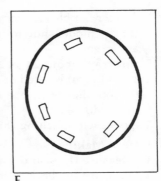

F

Stand

1. Lay the easel stand piece of matt board on a piece of fabric, doubled, with right sides together. Trace an outline.

2. Add 1/4" (0.6 cm) seam allowance and cut out.

3. Machine sew with a fine stitch (about 12 stitches to the inch or 2.5 cm).

4. Sew around three sides only, leaving the bottom edges open for turning.

5. Turn, poke out corners fully, press, and insert matt board.

6. With a fine whipstitch, handstitch the openings closed, turning the raw edges inside.

7. Glue the smallest end of the stand to the frame back and attach a small piece of ribbon as shown (E). Make sure the frame stands well.

8. Using the small "spacer" pieces, glue them around frame as shown and leave one side open so that the photograph can be put in and out (F).

9. Spread the glue along the other side of the spacers and place the front frame on top, being careful to align both frame pieces perfectly.

10. Weight with a heavy book and leave to dry overnight.

Note: Additional trims such as tiny artificial flowers, loose ribbons, shells, etc., can be glued on. If you are planning to hang the frame on the wall, a small plastic ring can be hand sewn to the back of the frame.

You may wish to make other types of frames. The following books are extremely helpful with specific instructions and patterns and can be found in quilt supply shops or ordered by mail. *Soft Sculpture Frames, Boxes and Baskets,* Craft Course Publishers, Walnut, California, 1981; *Fabric Frames,* Gick Publishing Inc., P.O. Box 2910, Laguna Hills, CA. 92653, 1980, written by Terri L. Gick and Pat Porter; and *Creative Fabric Frames,* Yours Truly, Inc., Box 80218, Atlanta, GA. 30366, 1981, written by Sally Paul. Precut frames for covering with fabric may be obtained by mail from *Frame-It,* Small Beginnings, Box 534, Markham, Ont. L3P 3R1; Home Arts Distribution, P.O. Box 3551, Orange, Ca. 92665; or Yours Truly, Inc., Box 80218, Atlanta, GA. 30366.

Crazy Patchwork Chair Pads

These colorful and reversible chair pads are easily made and they wash well. Choose bright colors to add a cheery note to your kitchen, family room, or cottage.

Technique Used   Modern materials machine method

Techniques Suitable   All

Materials Required

Foundation material (for one chair with two pads you will need 3/4 yd or 67.5 cm)

Polyester double knit scraps in cheerful colors to match the decor of the room
   (In the model shown, the colors are predominantly yellow, orange, brown, and green.)

Plain scraps about 24" x 24" (60 cm x 60 cm) for ties

1/2 yd (45 cm) bonded quilt or comforter batting, per chair
   (If you choose to use materials that could fray, use the semi-traditional method.)

1 spool each matching thread and contrasting sewing thread

Pattern Making

1. Measure the seat of the chair for which the pad is to be made.

2. Measure the back of the chair for which the pad is to be made.

3. Add 2" (5 cm) for seam allowance.

Cutting

1. Using these measurements, cut two foundation pieces for each pad.
2. Using these measurements, cut a double piece of batting for each pad.

Laying Out

1. On each foundation piece, lay out your scraps until you are satisfied with your composition.
2. Remember to start in a corner and work diagonally out and upwards.

Pinning and Basting

1. Pin in place and then baste if you feel you have to. Basting is not so important when you use this method and polyester scraps.

Embellishment

1. Machine sew either a satin stitch or decorative stitches, using a brightly contrasting sewing thread and being sure that the stitch catches both sides of the join to secure both patches. *Do not use a plain zigzag stitch* because it is not close enough for good wear.

Making Up

1. Lay out one pad piece, *face up,* for the back of the pad.
2. Lay the other piece, *face down,* on top of it.
3. Cover with the batting piece.
4. Starting in the centre of one side, machine sew around the pieces, leaving a 6" (15 cm) opening for turning.
5. Trim seams, notch corners, and turn.

Finishing

1. Using matching thread and a fine, close whipstitch, hand sew the opening closed.
2. Attach ties made from one of the plain pieces in the patchwork. Refer to page 50 for directions for making ties. They may be attached by hand or machine.
3. Tie the chair pad in the centre and in four other places using yarn to keep the batting from "clumping."

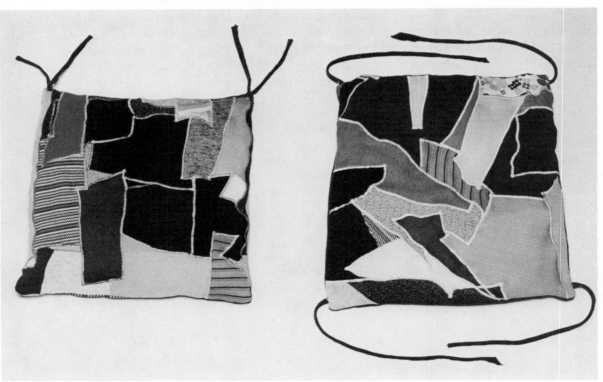

Crazy Patchwork Sewing Accessories

A few years ago, at The Great Canadian Quilting Bee in Victoria, B.C. in one of my workshops on crazy patchwork, I noticed one of the participants using a lovely sewing accessory set. Beulah Hodgson of Vancouver, Washington had designed this useful, practical set to show off her love of crazy patchwork and stitchery.

Ingeniously designed to be efficient and portable, the pincushion doll fits into its own pocket on the side of the tote bag and all the other accessories pack neatly inside, with ample room for "work in progress." Beulah used cottons for hers but you can use any materials you like.

Technique Used Traditional

Techniques Suitable All

Materials Required (for all the projects)

2-1/2 yds (2.5 m) prewashed muslin (often called "factory cotton" in Canada)
1/2 yd (45 cm) each of cotton or polyester/cotton blends in bright yellow, orange, rust, and green — some in plains and some in prints
1 yd (1 m) each of soft yellow, green, and aqua for the background
1-1/2 yds (1.5 m) of heavyweight pellon™ fleece, for body
1 spool sewing thread to match lining
1 spool dark green, dark aqua, or black sewing thread
1 spool each bright yellow, bright green, and rust #5 pearl cotton
1 spool each pale yellow and pale green #5 pearl cotton
1 package black, dark green, or dark aqua bias tape
Velcro fasteners and glue for pocket closures
2-1/2 yds (2.5 m) of lining fabric (should be one of the darker colors)

Tote Bag

The tote is a sampler of various techniques as well as an efficient and useful sewing accessory. Side (A) shows an original flower design that makes use of the "stained glass" quilting technique. Side (B) utilizes a pieced star motif based on a hexagon. End piece (C) is a piece of crazy patchwork that makes the pocket for the pincushion doll. End piece (D) makes use of a simple but lovely applique and embroidered motif on a crazy patchwork background. The straps are made of strip patchwork embellished with herringbone stitch.

Additional Materials Required

16-1/2" x 4-1/2" (41.25 cm x 11.25 cm) heavy cardboard for base
Lining material cut to fit above piece
17-1/2" x 5-1/2" (43.75 cm x 13.75 cm) vinyl bottom piece
1/8 yd (11.25 cm) of 1/4" (0.6 cm) elastic for pocket for doll

Pattern Making

1. Transfer the petal design onto a piece of tissue paper.
2. Go over lines with a black felt-tipped pen and let dry thoroughly.
3. Use under the foundation piece for side A and mark with marking pen.

Cutting

1. Cut out two pieces of foundation fabric each 15-1/2" x 17-1/2" (38.75 cm x 43.75 cm).
2. Cut out two lining pieces and two pellon pieces, same dimensions.
3. Cut out two straps from foundation material, each 27-1/2" x 2" (68.75 cm x 5 cm), also two pieces each (same dimensions) from pellon fleece and lining.
4. Cut one piece of foundation, one lining, one pellon for base, each 15" x 5" (37.5 cm x 12.5 cm) (E).

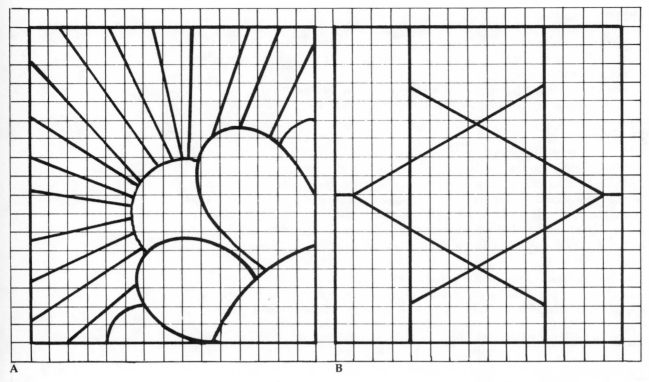

A   B

1 square = 1″ (2.5 cm)
Add 1/2″ (1.25 cm) seam allowance

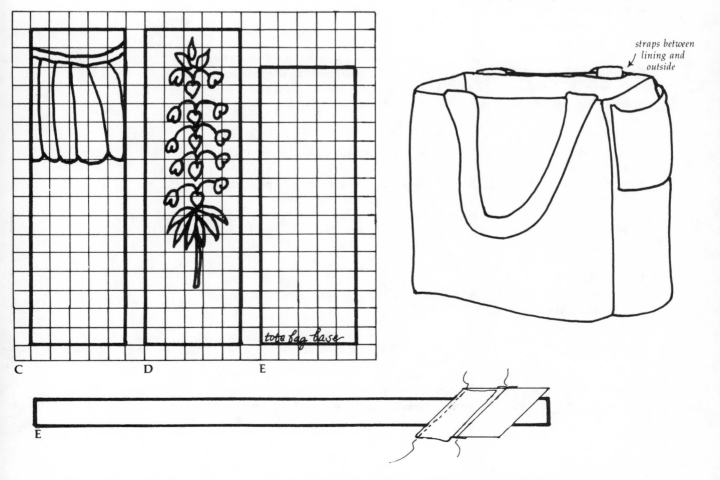

straps between
lining and
outside

tote bag base

C   D   E

E

Side A
Laying Out
1. Arrange lower left circle in bright green prints and solids, outer petals in bright yellow prints and solids, and background rays in a variety of soft yellow prints and plains.
2. Pin and baste in place when a pleasing order has been achieved.
3. Turn to page 16 for specific instructions on traditional-style crazy patchwork.

Embellishment
1. Use herringbone stitch, featherstitch, and all variations of these basic stitches. Check the section on stitches and let your imagination soar.
2. When the stitching is completed, working from the upper left corner towards the lower right corner, hand applique the dark green or black bias tape along the outer edges of the design. To do this, pin the inner edge of the curve in place and hand stitch; then stitch the longer, outer curve which will, because of being cut on the bias, stretch to accommodate the longer curve.

Side B
The design is a six-pointed star based on a hexagon. The points are solid colors and the hexagon is crazy patchwork in bright yellows, oranges, rusts, and greens. Choose softer shades of these colors for the background of the bag for contrast.

Pattern Making
1. Draft the star pattern full size.

Laying Out
1. Lay out the background first; pin and baste.
2. Put crazy patchwork on the hexagon and then piece plain star points to it, turning under raw edges all around, 1/2" (1.25 cm).
3. Baste in place.

Embellishment
1. Heavy, elaborate embroidery is needed on the star to make it stand out. Beulah used "needle lace" on the star point and cross-hatching with spider's web centres in the hexagon, but you can use any favorite stitches. Some suggestions are double herringbone, laced herringbone, vandyke stitch, broad chain, cable chain, zigzag chain, and woven spider's web.

End Piece C
This side piece is made in traditional crazy patchwork embroidery to match the front and back of the bag.
1. Cut a pocket 5-1/2" (13.75 cm) wide and 6" (15 cm) long of plain material.
2. Turn under a casing on the upper edge and machine stitch.
3. Insert elastic and tighten slightly to gather so that the doll will not fall out.
4. Machine or hand stitch in place across the bottom. Side seams will be caught in the seams of the tote.

End Piece D
Laying Out
1. Lay out pieces using softer shades of yellows, greens, rust, and aqua.
2. Pin and baste in place.

Embellishment
1. The plant design is adapted from an old quilt which was once displayed by the Portland, Oregon Historical Society.
2. The heart-shaped flowers are appliqued in rust floral print and held in place by buttonhole stitches in rust pearl cotton.
3. The stems and leaves are embroidered in green #5 pearl cotton.

Straps

These are strip-pieced by machine. One (in pastel greens and yellows) is used for the sunflower side and the other (in greens, yellows, rusts, and aqua) is for the brighter side.

Making Strip Piecing

1. Lay out the foundation strips, right side down; cover with quilt batt or fleece, and pin in place.
2. Lay one strip diagonally across the edge of the strip (E).
3. With right sides together, add another strip at an angle and machine sew in place.
4. Finger press open and pin in place.
5. Continue adding strips, machine stitching, opening, and pinning until the entire strip is covered; trim uneven edges.
6. With right side of lining piece and pieced strip together, using a 1/4" (0.6 cm) seam, machine sew, leaving one end open.
7. Turn and make sure corners are "poked out."
8. Turn in raw edges of open end and sew shut neatly by hand or machine.

Finishing

1. Baste pellon fleece to the inside of the lining pieces for the body of the bag.
2. If pockets are desired on the lining, construct them in the same way that the outer pocket for the doll was made.
3. Flap pockets can be made by sewing the pocket itself to the lining and attaching a flap. Glue or sew a matching velcro fastener to the flap and pocket.
4. This tote had pockets for the needle case, scissor cases, and the sundry sewing items Beulah customarily uses.
5. Measure outer pieces (sometimes they "shrink" slightly in the stitching); trim lining to the same size.
6. Attach side A to side strip C, and side piece B to side piece D.
7. Assemble base wrong sides together, turn, press.
8. Matching carefully at corners, pin the base piece to side A, and pin carefully all along the sides.
9. Repeat with side piece B.
10. Assemble the lining in the same manner but leave about a 4" (10 cm) opening in the base pieces.

11. Turn both the outer shell of the tote and the lining inside out.

12. Slip the lining inside the patchwork shell so right sides are together.

13. Pin the shell and lining together at the top.

14. Insert the straps between the lining and the outer shell so they will be caught in the top seam.

15. Machine sew around the top edges.

16. Turn (through the opening left for this purpose), and press.

17. Close the openings neatly by hand.

18. You may want to tack the side seams of the lining and the outside of the shell together to prevent "slippage."

Doll Pincushion

The pattern for the 8-1/2" (21.25 cm) doll which is the basis of this pincushion is a copyright pattern by Margie Hadley of *Pebbles 'n Patches,* 6005 NE 47th Street, Vancouver, Washington 98661. It can be purchased for $1.50 (US funds).

Technique Used   Traditional

Technique Suitable   Traditional

Additional Materials Required

1/2 yd (45 cm) unbleached muslin (also known as "factory cotton" in Canada) prewashed, to be used for the foundation pattern

Scraps of cotton to match tote bag

Yellow, green, rust #5 pearl embroidery cotton

Bran or dried coffee grounds for stuffing doll

Scraps of yarn for hair

Commercial "strawberry," if desired

Pattern Making

1. Any two-dimensional doll pattern with skirt attached can be adapted to this technique. Draw the outline of the doll on the foundation fabric with water-soluble markers or light pencil lines.

Laying Out

1. Use small-scale patches for best effect and follow the contours of the neck, skirt, and sleeves.

2. Pin in place and baste.

Embellishment

1. Use simple, small-scale stitches in keeping with the size of the piece.

2. Solid patches can be decorated with french knots, spanish knots, and bullion stitches.

3. Embroider features on face of doll.

Cutting

1. Cutting out, allowing a 1/2" (1.25 cm) seam allowance.

Making Up

1. With right sides together, sew seams by machine or hand sew with a very small stitch.

2. Turn, press, and work over the seamlines with a variety of your favorite stitches.

3. Stuff tightly. Quilt batting can be used but will ultimately dull your pins. Bran or dried coffee grounds are a better choice.

4. Complete the construction by adding yarn hair and if desired a mobcap made from a circle of fabric.

5. A commercial "strawberry" can be attached at the back for sharpening your needles and pins.

Needle Case

Technique Used   Traditional

Technique Suitable   Traditional

Additional Materials Required

5 squares of wool felt or good quality wool material

Pinking shears

2 pieces of 1/4" (0.6 cm) wide grosgrain ribbon each 7" (17.5 cm) long

Cutting

1. Cut three pieces 11" x 7" (27.5 cm x 17.5 cm) (F). Cut one of foundation fabric, one of pellon fleece, and one of lining.

2. Cut five pieces of wool felt with pinking shears 10" x 6" (25 cm x 15 cm).

Laying Out

1. Lay out scraps in a pleasing design; pin and baste. Scraps should be no bigger than 3" (7.5 cm).

Embellishment

1. Use a variety of stitches and embroider the word "Needles" in backstitch on a plain patch.

Making Up

1. Place the right sides of the embellished piece and the right side of the lining together.

2. Add the pellon fleece on top.

3. Machine stitch with 1/4" (0.6 cm) seams from X around to Y on diagram (G), starting and stopping securely, leaving 4" (10 cm) open for turning.

4. Notch corners, clip seams, and turn.

5. Turn in the seams at the opening and hand stitch closed.

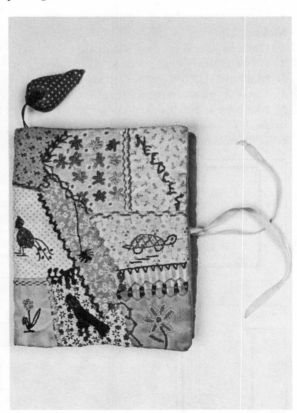

Finishing

1. Centre the five wool pieces (pages) on lining of needle case.
2. Using pearl cotton, backstitch by hand through and along the centre of all pieces. Keep checking to see that you are keeping your stitches in a neat, straight line on the outer case.
3. You can lace through the backstitch on the right side with a different colored embroidery thread.
4. Label the wool "pages" with the type of needle you intend to place there —crewel, tapestry, quilting, embroidery, sewing needles, etc.
5. Sew a length of ribbon on the centre of front and back for ties.

Scissor Cases

Additional Materials Required

Velcro dots and glue for closing cases

Pattern Making

1. Trace around your scissors, adding about 3/4" (1.8 cm) for seam allowance, and ease. Diagram (I) is an average size for scissors. Adjust as required.

Cutting

1. Using the above pattern, cut a back and front for each case in foundation material.
2. Cut two pieces of pellon fleece and two lining pieces.

Laying Out

1. Lay out the patchwork pieces on the foundation materials in a pleasing design.
2. Pin and baste in place.

Embellishment

1. Use a variety of your favorite stitches.

Making Up

1. Place back and front of cases together, right sides together.
2. Add a pellon fleece piece to each side and pin in place.
3. Machine stitch together on sides and bottom using 1/4" (0.6 cm) seams.
4. Clip curves and notch corners, then turn.
5. Machine stitch lining pieces, right sides together, on the sides and bottom using 1/4" (0.6 cm) seams.
6. Clip, notch, turn, and press.

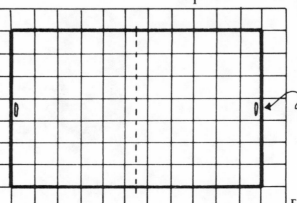

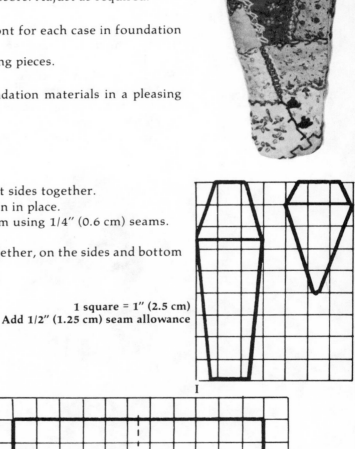

1 square = 1" (2.5 cm)
Add 1/2" (1.25 cm) seam allowance

I

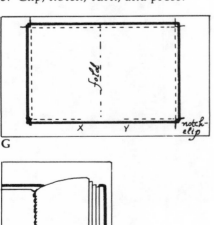

G

H

1 square = 1" (2.5 cm)
Add 1/2" (1.25 cm)
seam allowance

attach ribbons here

F

7. Slip lining into case, wrong sides together, and pin in place.

8. Hand stitch the upper seams, turning raw edges in.

Finishing

1. Glue velcro dots in place or use hooks and eyes and sew them in place with matching thread.

Thread Box

Technique Used   Traditional

Technique Suitable   Traditional

Pattern Making

1. Using the diagram given, draw the pattern, including all design and marking lines (J).

2. Go over all lines with a black felt-tipped pen and allow to dry thoroughly.

3. Place design under the foundation fabric and lightly draw in all details with an HB pencil or water-soluble pen.

Cutting

1. Cut out one pattern of foundation fabric, one of pellon fleece, and one of lining, allowing 1/2" (1.25 cm) seam allowances all around.

Laying Out

1. Bases of the fans are the darkest solid color. Pin and baste in place.

2. Backgrounds of the pieces may be strip pieced, using softer shades of your chosen color.

3. Add the plain patch for the bottom of the box.

4. Lay out brightest colors in the fan shape; pin and baste.

5. Using the same color as the fan base, make a narrow bias strip to outline ribs of fan and outer edge.

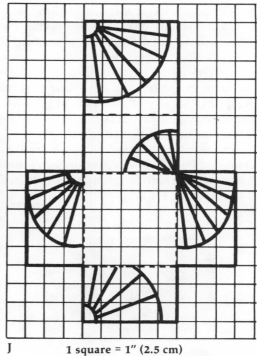

J   **1 square = 1" (2.5 cm)**
Add 1/2" (1.25 cm) seam allowance

Embellishment

1. On the lighter strip sections use fancy stitching between the strips but keep the threads in the same lighter tones.
2. On the crazy patch detail use green, bright yellow, and rust #5 pearl cotton and a rich variety of ornate stitches.

Making Up

1. Place the right side of the embroidered outer shell and the right side of the lining together.
2. Top with pellon fleece.
3. Machine stitch together leaving a 1/2" (1.25 cm) seam allowance all around except for the top edge which is left open for turning.
4. Trim seams, notch corners, and clip inner corners.
5. Turn and press lightly.
6. Machine or hand stitch along fold lines.

Finishing

1. Turn in raw edge of top and hand stitch closed.
2. Fold sides up and hand stitch sides with small overcast stitch.
3. Attach ribbon ties to lid and front so box can be tied closed.

Crazy Patchwork Stickpin Cushion   (Two Variations)

This is a delightful addition to milady's boudoir. One lady of my acquaintance used the scraps from her mother's bridesmaid's gowns and wedding gown to make a delightfully nostalgic gift for her mother. In a more subdued version, gentlemen will find it handy for keeping their tiepins.

Technique Used   Traditional

Technique Suitable   Traditional

Materials Required

6" (15 cm) square of soft foundation fabric

6" (15 cm) square of royal blue backing (cotton sateen or silk)

Several cupfuls of dried coffee grounds for stuffing (You may use bran flakes if you like but that may encourage "critters." If you use scraps of quilt batting, be aware that over the course of time your brooches and pins will become dull on the points and snag your clothing.)

Scraps in a variety of materials in royal blues and oranges

1 spool orange #8 pearl cotton

Royal blue sewing thread

Scraps of velvet in all colors, not more than 2" (5 cm)

Odds and ends of colored, stranded cotton or silk embroidery floss

A piece of blue cotton, satin, or silk to match the backing, 36" (90 cm) long by 2" (5 cm) wide, for frill

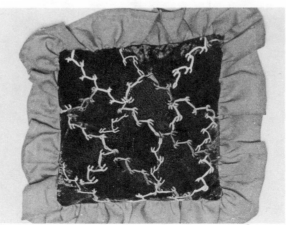

A   B

Pattern Making

No pattern is required for this project.

Laying Out

1. Lay out the scraps in a pleasing order starting at the lower left corner and working up and across the square. Tie silk, dress silks, and fine corduroy are used in the two variations shown here.

Pinning and Basting

1. Continue, follow directions for the traditional technique.

Embellishment

1. The stitches used for pin cushion A are closed buttonhole, open cretan stitch, triple featherstitch, open and closed herringbone stitch, rosette chain stitch, and detached and attached fly stitch.
2. The stitch used in pin cushion B is featherstitch worked in various colors which gives quite a different effect.

Making Up

1. Press and block the embellished squares; trim if necessary.
2. Cut a blue sateen backing using the front as a pattern; be sure it is square.
3. *Pin Cushion A* Seam together three-and-a-half sides as shown. Turn, push out the corners, and fill.
4. Hand stitch the opening closed with tiny overcast stitches in royal blue sewing thread.
5. *Pin Cushion B* Make a narrow hand or machine stitched hem on the ruffle strip.
6. Gather to fit the square. (A ruffler attachment for your sewing machine is a real help here.)
7. Pin the ruffle to the front of the pin cushion with right sides together and stitch.
8. With the ruffle to the inside, pin the front and back of the pin cushion together and sew around three-and-a-half sides.
9. Turn, pull out corners, and press lightly.

Finishing

1. Fill with the dry coffee grounds and sew the opening closed with tiny overcast stitches in royal blue.

Toilet Seat Cover and Guest Towels

Designed by Jeanne Warwick for her guest powder room, this ensemble is an elegant way to "pull together" the elements and colors in your decor. Team the set with the wall piece "Victoriana memorabilia" to hang over the toilet for a stunning effect.

Technique Used   Traditional

Techniques Suitable   All

Materials Required

1/2 yd (45 cm) quilt batting (if using padded methods)

1/2 yd (45 cm) medium-weight foundation fabric

Scraps of fabrics for patchwork — Jeanne used black velvet and multicolored cottons that emphasized red, green, yellow, and some blue

1 spool gold-colored #5 or #8 pearl cotton

1/2 yd (45 cm) lining material

1 yd (1 m) woven tape (purchase in notions department)

1/4 yd (22.5 cm) plain cotton in your predominant dark color (black)

2-1 yd (1 m) pieces of wax paper

Masking tape or scotch tape

Pattern Making

1. Tape together the two pieces of wax paper, side by side.
2. Lay it over your toilet seat lid and tape it down all around.
3. Crease the shape of the toilet lid into the paper by running your finger firmly around the edges of it.
4. Add 3" (7.5 cm) all around and cut out for your pattern. (This includes seam allowances and an allowance for the stitches "taking up" extra material.)

Cutting

1. Cut out the shape in the foundation material and in the lining material.
2. If you are using one of the techniques that uses padding, cut out the shape in batting.

Laying Out

1. On the foundation piece, lay out the scraps until you have a pleasing collage. (If using a machine technique, remember to applique some curved shapes for interest in your design.)
2. Be sure to balance your plains and prints, darks and lights.

Pinning and Basting

1. Pin and/or baste as your method requires.

Embellishment

1. This is one place to allow your imagination full play with fancy stitches and combinations. Refer to the stitch section for stitches and stitch combinations. The seat cover shown uses plain chain stitch; detached chains arranged as flowers; blanket stitch and various combinations including detached and attached fly stitch; cross-stitch; herringbone stitch in several variations; fly stitch combination II and III; star stitch; backstitch; and flat stitch combinations II and III. (Jeanne added her initials and the date in backstitch on a plain patch.)
2. Press work, face down, on a turkish towel; trim any edges that hang over.
3. Check cover for size and shape on the toilet seat it is to cover; adjust where necessary.

Making Up

1. Lay cover face down and cover with the lining material, right side up.
2. Machine stitch around the edges to hold it together.
3. Using a 2-1/2" (6.25 cm) wide strip of black cotton, make a casing all around by putting the wrong side of the casing to the right raw edge of the cover and machine sew.
4. Turn to the inside, press seam, and machine sew "in-the-ditch" to create the casing (A).
5. Thread the tape through the casing by pinning a medium-sized safety pin to one end and work through.

Note: This pert cover is lovely made in ginghams and prints in one color with some white or colored eyelet using the semi-traditional with variation I technique. You can add an eyelet ruffle for an especially feminine effect. Black and white or blue and white are especially crisp looking.

Towels

Jeanne used some antique yellow linen hand towels and decorated them with flower motifs cut from crazy patchwork which she appliqued in place with a fine whipstitch. You can use a close herringbone stitch or blanket stitch for a more decorative effect. If antique linen hand towels are not available use plain terry towels in a harmonizing color decorated with motifs cut from crazy patchwork.

.Note: Cut your pattern for the motif from paper and pin it in place on the patchwork and then stitch *around (not on) the motif with a fine machine stitch (12 stitches to the inch or 2.5 cm) to stabilize the patchwork. Remove the paper and cut just outside the stitching, leaving enough material to turn under.*

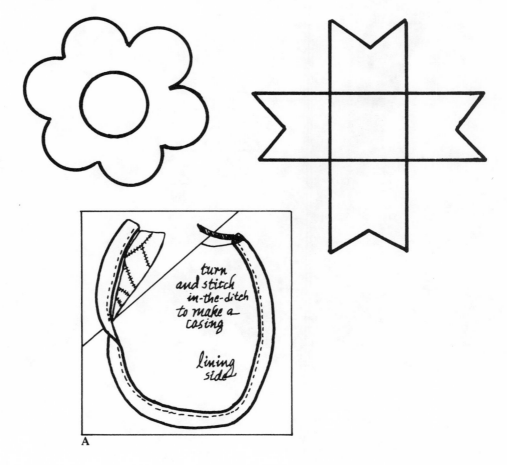

turn and stitch in-the-ditch to make a casing

lining side

A

Bible Bookmark and Wedding Guest Bookmarkers

Make the wedding memorable with matching Bible and guest bookmarkers. Easily made, they are treasured mementos of that important day. I used the materials from the wedding party gowns. This had great sentimental value for me. But you could choose materials to highlight the decor of the church or synagogue.

Follow the directions for making crazy patchwork strips given in the directions for the wedding dress on pages 74, 75 and work a strip 6" (15 cm) long.

Making Up

1. Measure the length of the book (open) and add 1" (2.5 cm) for finishing plus 6" (15 cm) for the worked section and cut a length of satin or grosgrain ribbon 2" (5 cm) wide.

2. Attach the worked strip to one end, wrong sides together, and with a very tiny whipstitch in burgundy or pink turn under the raw edges and join together.

3. Loop the unworked end and attach to top end of worked piece so that it can be just slipped over the open Bible or guest book.

Finishing

1. Using either pink, burgundy, or turquoise #8 pearl cotton, make individual fringe knots very close together with ends about 1" (2.5 cm) long. Secure each one individually.

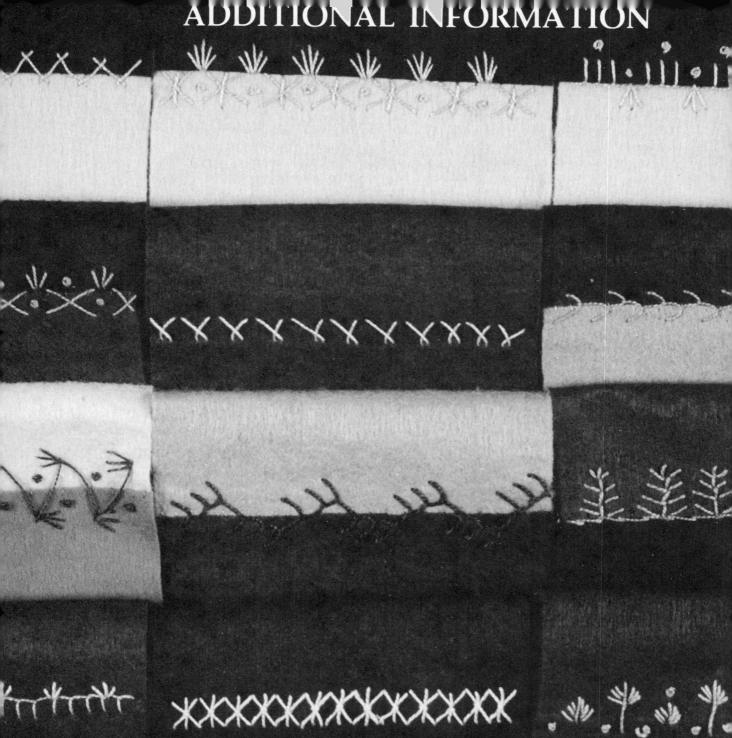

Caring for Old Crazy Patchwork Quilts

Most of the information given here is for silk quilts, but the general discussion pertains to old cottons and wools as well. Of course some of the silk-like materials in later crazy quilts may well be rayon. Rayon was the first synthetic fibre to be produced and was discovered in 1855 by G. Audemars. It was called "artificial silk." Since it does not wear well it benefits from the same type of care given to fragile silks. Because old textiles deteriorate almost as quickly when stored as when *carefully* displayed it is just as well to keep them in view if you enjoy them.

Cleaning

Dirt, especially dust, destroys silk and other fibres by cutting them and in some cases forming permanent stains with moisture and dyes. To wash silk in any crazy patchwork usually causes great damage. The dyes, mordants, and weighting substances plus the chemicals used to restore the "scroop" (the rustle and lustre of silk) often combine with water and run into other parts of the quilt, staining them. Water also spots silk by partially dissolving the animal gums applied to restore the body to silks. These spots are virtually impossible to remove. Dry-cleaning solvents, even professional types, are very harmful to silks for all of the reasons stated above.

The best way to clean crazy work pieces is to tie a piece of fine cheesecloth over one of the small attachments (upholstery tool, etc.) of your vacuum cleaner. Lay the quilt out flat, preferably raising it a few inches off the flat surface so that the air can circulate. Holding the vacuum nozzle just *above the piece,* gently vacuum first the front and then the back. Much accumulated dirt can be removed this way.

Because the silk fabrics are so delicate prevention of soiling and damage are the best ways to care for your old quilt. Handle it as little as possible and wash your hands before handling because oil from the skin is damaging. Do not smoke, eat, or drink near the textile. Do not place anything on crazy patchwork.

Storing and Displaying

There is no perfect way to store or display textiles but some ways are better than others.

Displaying

According to Professor Michael M. Bogle, conservator at the Merrimack Valley Textile Museum, silks produced in the 19th and early 20th centuries are rapidly deteriorating. In part this is due to the strong mordants used for dyeing. These mordants (substances which, by combining with a dyestuff, form an insoluble compound which produce a fixed color in a textile fibre) were mostly metal salts, usually tin, which have altered the acid or alkaline content of the silk producing increased brittleness and rapid breakdown of fibres. Another contributing factor is the "weighting" that some silks received to permit the proper draping of the silk as well as treatment with acetic acid to restore the rustle or "scroop" of the silk that was removed by the dyeing and finishing processes.

Fluorescent light and sunlight are the worst enemies of old silk. Any bright household lighting is harmful so when displaying your treasured antique, choose a spot where light can be kept dim by using low-level artificial light and drawing draperies. As well, keep it away from heat sources such as radiators, fireplaces, and heat vents. Gases from gas heating also fade silks.

Rooms that are kept at 60° F to 65° F help to preserve silk fibres and can be comfortable for humans.

Hanging

It is important to distribute the weight of the piece evenly and to support it. Fabrics supported by another fabric or by a surface last more than twice as long as unsupported fabrics.

Hand sew a "sleeve" (A) to the back of the piece, preferably top and bottom, and support with rods. Taking the piece up and down frequently is also hard on it. You will hear the brittle stitches and fabric breaking each time you do it and it will break your heart!

Framing

Framing textiles can be successful if it is done with care. I have personally seen the tragic results when textile pieces were poorly protected by ill-fitting glass. Dust, oils, and other pollutants from the air, especially smoke, combine with moisture behind the glass, and all conspire to rot the piece. You can frame a small piece of a precious crazy quilt, which is otherwise unusable. This is a nice way to preserve the patchwork and its memories and share them with family members. I prefer to have the piece framed without glass and to vacuum it as I have described. The framing process also permits the rich texture of the stitches to be appreciated and this is a great part of patchwork's appeal. Be sure to use acid-free matting cardboard and refrain from using glues and tacks on the piece. The backing can be covered with acid-free paper which also lends support to the piece.

Folding

Crazy patchwork pieces may be folded for display and storage, but they should be refolded at three-month intervals along different fold lines. Displaying a folded piece on an upholstered surface is relatively harmless but do not place the piece on wood; oils and acid in the wood may interact with the dyes and destroy the fibres.

Storing

Do not wrap crazy quilts in plastic. The plastic traps moisture which interacts with the dyes and accumulated soil to hasten deterioration. Muslin is probably the best choice. I prefer well-washed old sheeting loosely wrapped around the quilt. If using tissue paper, make sure it is an acid-free type. Rolling in muslin or acid-free tissue paper on rods or rolls covered with the same can be done carefully and this method protects against wear along creases. Do not stack many quilts one on top of the other. The underneath ones will suffer from the pressure. The same is true for rolled quilts; they are better suspended (B) or stood on end (C). Do not tie bundles of textiles in their protective shrouding.

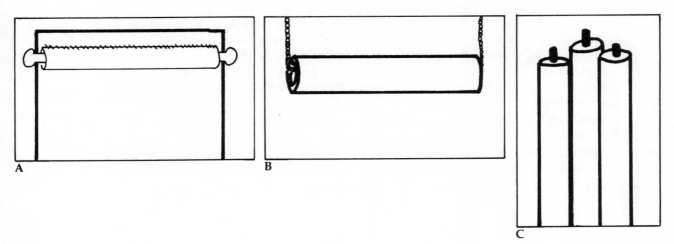

A   B   C

This places pressure on fibres and breaks them. If possible, store quilts flat, covered with protective muslin or paper. Most households will suffer little damage from pests but a few moth balls in the storage place (not in contact with the quilts) will discourage this pest.

Repairing Old Crazy Patchwork

To prevent further deterioration of silks that have split and frayed it is sometimes desirable to repair them. Keep in mind that adding anything to an antique quilt detracts from its value so any repair should be done infrequently and only if further damage will result if the repair is not done.

Museum conservators use "crepeline" which is fine, sheer fabric made especially for textile conservation work. However, silk organza in the appropriate color is a good substitute but may also be difficult to locate. I like to use fine silk tulle which is more readily available. Proceed with your repair by covering the patch with matching fine tulle. With fine whipstitching using thread of compatible weight and fibre and a fine needle, sew the patch to the edge of the old patch at or near the seamline which is usually the strongest point of the old patch. Occasionally, if I can find appropriate embroidery silks, I will repair some of the embroidery if this is necessary.

If you are interested in repairing and restoring old patchwork quilts you may wish to refer to some of the books in the following list.

Bogle, Michael M. with Finch, Karen, (Hampton Court Palace, England), *Technical Data on Silk Textiles*, Textile Conservation Centre Notes, #1, Publications Department, Merrimack Valley Museum, Andover, Mass., 1979.

Bogle, Michael M., with Leene, Jentina E., Laboratory for Textile Technology, University of Delft, Delft, The Netherlands, *Technical Data on Rayon*, Textile Conservation Centre Notes, #7, Publications Department, Merrimack Valley Museum, Andover, Mass., 1979.

Bogle, Michael M., with Zeronian, S. Haig, Professor of Textile Science, University of California, Davis, Ca., *Technical Data on Acetate, Triacetate, Nylon and Polyester*, Textile Conservation Centre Notes, #8, Publications Department, Merrimack Valley Museum, Andover, Mass., 1979.

Bogle, Michael, M. with Morrison, Robert C., School of Applied Science, Canberra College of Advanced Education, Belconnen, Australia, *The Deterioration of Silks Through Artificial Weighting*, Textile Conservation Centre Notes, #11, Publications Department, Merrimack Museum, Andover, Mass., 1979.

Bogle, Michael M. with Koob, Katherine R., *Museum Display of Textiles*, Textile Conservation Centre Notes, #13, Publications Department, Merrimack Valley Museum, Andover, Mass., 1979.

Bogle, Michael M. with Clark, Karen, Textile Conservation Workshop, New Salem, N.Y., *The Storage of Textiles*, Textile Centre Notes, #14, Publications Department, Merrimack Valley Museum, Andover, Mass., 1979.

Bogle, Michael M., *Mounting of Textiles for Storage and Display*, Textile Conservation Centre Notes, #15, Publications Department, Merrimack Valley Museum, Andover, Mass., 1979.

Guldbeck, Per E., *The Care of Historical Collections*, American Association for State and Local History, Nashville, Tenn., 1972.

Maitland, Harold F., *Considerations for the Care of Textiles and Costumes*, Indianapolis Museum of Art, Indianapolis, Indiana, 1980.

Sommer, Elyse, *The Textile Collector's Guide*, Sovereign Books, New York, 1978.

Antique Crazy Patchwork Panels and Cushion Top

On principle, I consider it a desecration to cut up any quilt, old or new, that is in reasonably good condition. However, if you have the good fortune to own a crazy quilt that is worn beyond using or is unusable for some other reason, and would like to preserve and display it, this is one way to do it.

A crazy patchwork quilt top was given to me to "do something with" for the annual church fair. Realizing that the donor did not know the value of his grandmother's work I offered to repair the quilt and make it into two wall hangings and two cushions for the man's two children. The top was quite small consisting of four 12" (30 cm) squares across and six squares down. Four of these were the same size as the others but several were constructed of smaller squares worked together to build up the required size. The embroidery was exquisite and in good repair but certain silk pieces were rotting. The entire piece was of brilliant plain and novelty-woven silks in hot pinks, black, navy, lighter pink, royal blue, fuschia, pale blue, grey, red, mauve, and a little olive green. On one side was embroidered the date "1900" and on the other "1901," presumably the starting and finishing dates.

The construction of the quilt top was interesting. A variety of heavy cottons and lightweight wools had been used for the foundation fabrics for the squares. A thin layer of uncarded wool was spread over these and the silks laid down over this and the stitchery worked through to the back. The silk threads were twisted and about the weight of #8 pearl cotton. Colors of yellow, green, pale blue, royal blue, green, gold, orange, pink, red in all shades were used with great effect. The patches were not embellished with motifs other than a few scattered star stitches on the larger patches.

I carefully ripped out the stitches with a seam ripper and repaired it where necessary. Then I took off one row of irregular blocks at the bottom end, and divided the top into two panels, each with one of the dates on it.

I chose gold-colored broadcloth to line the panels. The panels of lining were cut 1" (2.5 cm) larger all around and the raw edges of the panel and lining were turned in. I used good quality pins to hold the pieces and did not leave them in too long to damage the fabric.

Using a very fine, close whipstitch with gold-colored cotton thread I attached the lining to the panel. Next I made a hand-stitched sleeve in the lining only, wide enough to accommodate the rods the owner planned to use. Rod hanging is necessary so that the weight of the work is evenly distributed. This way the pieces are well supported so that the stitches and fibres do not break.

Pillows

These are strictly for "show" since the material and stitching are much too delicate for use. However, they do complement the hangings. I cut a piece of gold-colored cotton broadcloth 1" (2.5 cm) larger all around than the pillow piece. I turned in the raw edges and sewed as described above, leaving a 3" (7.5 cm) opening on one side for stuffing. Polyester filling is more suitable than quilt batting to stuff the pillows, and this is what I used, making sure not to overstuff. Finally, I whipstitched the opening closed. The owner gave me the remaining pieces of crazy patchwork and I treasure them greatly.

Mail Order Supply Sources

Canada

The following shops have mail order service and are most obliging if you write and describe your needs. Send a stamped, self-addressed envelope for a reply. Usually, they place you on their catalogue list.

Gina Brown Needlecraft Studio
1230-A 17 Avenue
Calgary, Alberta
T2T 0B8

Hummingbird House
300 Lakeshore Road West
Mississauga, Ontario
L5H 1G6

The Good Wool Shop
1103 Corydon
Winnipeg, Manitoba
R3M 0X3

One Stitch At a Time
366 Adelaide St. E.
Toronto, Ontario

Vi-Elle's Needlecraft Supplies
 and Bernina Sewing Centre
3625 Weston Road, Unit 8
Weston, Ontario
M9L 1V9 *or*
Box 87, Station T
Toronto, Ontario
M6B 3Z9

United States

Treadleart
Department FA
2030 Velez Drive
San Pedro, Ca.
90732

Clearbrook Woolen Shop
Clearmont, Vermont
22624

Pure China Silk Company
RR #2, Box 70
Holdege, Nebraska
68949

This shop has different Ultrasuede™ scraps suitable for crazy patchwork. Write to them for prices and availability of colors.

You may wish to purchase a *Sewing Directory and Catalog Sources,* by Margaret A. Boyd (Bestway Publishing, 3511 Rushing Road, Augusta, Ga. 30906), for further mail order sources.

Index